JACOBITES OF 1715
North East Scotland

and

JACOBITES OF 1745
North East Scotland

by
Frances McDonnell

CLEARFIELD

Jacobites of 1715 originally published
St. Andrews, Scotland, 1996

Jacobites of 1745 originally published
St. Andrews, Scotland, 1996

Reprinted, two books in one, for
Clearfield Company by
Genealogical Publishing Co.
Baltimore, Maryland
1997, 1998, 2000, 2008

ISBN-13: 978-0-8063-4685-4
ISBN-10: 0-8063-4685-X

Made in the United States of America

JACOBITES of 1715
North East Scotland

by

Frances McDonnell

"They shook hands with ruin for what they esteemed the Cause of their King and country."

Robert Burns in a letter to Lady Winifred Maxwell Constable, 16 December 1789

"My Dearest

The hurry we are in and the crowd of Visitants since we came here hinders. I cannot at present give you a full account of me and fellow-prisoners I would otherwise.

It is enough to tell you in a general that in our progress to this place we have suffered the most barbarous and inhuman treatment ever was heard of in a Christian Country, and have been exposed in all the townes we have travelled thro' to all the mock pomp and outrage could be offered to Clergyman. Yet God was with us and has strengthened and upheld us; so that at the time, we are all in good habit and health. From Aberdeen we came that night to Stonehaven, being each of us on the road guarded by a Dutch soldier, riding two together, who died a long thong of leather to our bits, and hal'd us and drove us as they pleased.

At Stonehaven, after they had kept us a long time upon the Streets, we were shut up altogether into their prison house, a thieves' hole, and were like to be stifled for want of air. We got in at last some straw and tumbled down together like so many pigs in a hogsty.

I cannot ever forget the kindness of the inhabitants to us who brought us in blankets and clean linen Dr Garden and I, who have been inseparable companions in this doleful progresse, lay together in a corner and were easie, and resolved by God's grace to suffer the worst could befall us with ane undaunted courage.

When we came to Montrose about four in the afternoon, we were detained on horseback at the Cross a long long hour ere we were ordered to our jail, the whole town and wondering crowd gazing upon us, some God forgive them laughing and flouting at us, but the greatest part wringing their hands and shedding vollies of tears for us. At length, tho' they had ane upper prison, we were condemned, as if we had been the worst of malefactors, to a low dungeon, where we were so crowded, that we had scarce room to sit or stand, and no thing allowed us to sit down upon, and a long time before we could have any to clean and sweep the hole

Saturday, Aprile 7th - We came at night to Arbroath, where we were yet worse used, thrust into the worst jail I think in the kingdom - twenty one of us in number - a nasty filthy hole where we had nothing to sit upon, but an old bier upon which they carry out prisoners and poor people to the grave. Here we were kept five long hours ere we could have either meat or drink, though we had fasted all the day.

Yet even here our good God did not forsake us, but stirred up the compassion of a deal of good women who sent us in some bottles of ale and furnished us with bedclothes - particularly we were bound to Dr Burnett's wife's sister, Mrs Reid, who was very kind to us

Sunday, Aprile 8th. - We travelled to Dundee, and came there about the ringing of the last bell to afternoon preaching. We were held upon the street a long hour, the
. . and derision of the whiggish mob of that town, and at last put in prison, the best I believe in the nation, where we had a large gallerie to walk in, and got in

bedding. Here the good women and citizens showed a deal of kindness   I here again turned very unwell and was seized with the most racking fit of the collick, but praised be God, after midnight I turned wonderful easier. Here we stayed Monday all day which rested us.

Tuesday, Aprile 10th - We travelled to Cupar in Fife and there we met Cupar justice indeed! after a deal of indignities and insulting over us, by the ill natured mob while we waited at the Cross   We were thrust into the nastiest and narrowest vaults imaginable,   our troop of prisoners being now become very numerous by the accession of a deal of Angus gentlemen

Wednesday - We were carried to Kirkcaldy, through all the little towns of Fife on the road as a Rareshow.

Thursday - We crossed the Forth at Kinghorn.   About 3 o'clock we landed at Leith, amidst a vast concourse of people, and were forced up on foot to travel from Leith to Edinburgh, driven on like so many sacrifices, allowing us no time to halt for breath. I must say with my crippled leg, I thought I never to have got it done, but to have sunk under it, but God supported and strengthened me   We were brought through Leith Wynd and up the High Street to the Mainguard, the whole town viewing us, a glorious parade and triumphal band, while a great many (more) could hardly be kept from rabbling our guard, at the uncouth and lamentable sight   From the mainguard we were ordered to march back down the Canongate, where a deal of gentlemen came with us were put in prison - others and among them we of the Clergy were, with the gentlemen who voluntarily surrendered, put into Winton House in the Canongate, where we of the Clergy had a room to ourselves, five of us together, high and well aired, with a window to the Fore Street

We have got in very good bedding and our accommodation here is gentle

Thus, my dear, I have given you a short account of our progresse how long we may stay here God knows, for reports about us are very various, but it appears we are not like to get out in haste   However I hope all shall be well   God be thanked we are once got out of the hands of Swiss and Dutch.   Deliver me and all good men from harrassment as we have suffered from their boisterous officers

My blessing to you and all my children and loved Parishoners.

Let me hear from you.   I am to death yours

Letter from John Alexander, Minister of the Church of Scotland, to his wife.

Jacobites of 1715
North East Scotland

Abercromby, Alexander of Brunston or Brunstone
The Poll Book of 1696 gives Alexander Abercrombie, gentleman in Brunstone, Kinoir, his wife, and Thomas, Elizabeth, and Agnes his children. He survived the Rising of 1715 for many years.

Abercromby, Alexander, younger of Cothal
Son of Thomas Abercromby of Cothal, sometime of Collyhill, in Bourtie, who was brother to Alexander Abercromby of Fetternear, and son of Hector Abercromby of Fetternear and Marjory Gordon of Leicheston, his wife. Born in 1662, he went to Douai in 1677 aged 15, being then called the son of "D. Thomas of Fetterneir and Isobel Bisset of Lessendrum, sister of Fr. George Bisset." He did not become a priest but returned home and is described as "pius et ingeniousus adolescens."

Abercromby, George
Son of Alexander Abercromby of Nether Skeith, Banffshire. One of the sixteen heritors of Banffshire who surrendered at Banff in March 1716.

Abercromby, Sir James of Birkenbog
Born 1669 eldest son of Sir Alexander Abercromby and Elizabeth Baird

Abercromby, Sir James, Bart. of Birkenbog
Second baronet of Birkenbog, being the eldest son of Sir Alexander and his third wife, Elizabeth, daughter of Sir James Baird of Auchmedden. Sir James Abercromby, born about 1669, was MP for Banffshire from 1693 to 1702. He married Mary, daughter of Arthur Gordon of Straloch, and dying in September 1734 was succeeded by his third son Robert

Abercromby, John, of the Skeith family
Very little is known about him, not even the names of his parents. All that is certain is that Mar was joined in Perth on 4 Oct 1715 by Lachlan, 20th chief of Mackintosh with a regiment raised mostly from his own clan, in which "J.A. of the Skeith family" was one of his lieutenants, his ADC. (He may have been the same man as JA who on 29 June 1716 was, as "a rebel," put on board the ship *Elizabeth and Anne* at Liverpool, for Virginia).

Abercromby, John, of Authorsk (Aquhorsk or Afforsk)
Was the second son of Alexander of Fetternear, by his wife, Jean Seton of Newark, born 1655. His elder brother was Francis

Abercromby of Fetternear, created Lord Glasford, and the younger was Patrick, author of the *Martial Achievements of the Scottish Nation*

Abercromby, Patrick, Dr

Author of *Martial Achievements of the Scottish Nation*, was the third son of Alexander Abercromby of Fetternear and his wife, Jean Seton, and was born in 1656. At the age of fourteen he was sent to Douai and spent much of his youth at foreign Universities Took his degree as Doctor of Medicine at St Andrews in 1685 and appointed physician to James II

Abercromby, Stewart

A clergyman's son He came to an untimely end as outlined by a letter written by John Alexander, the painter, from Rome, dated 17 August 1718. "Mr Hay, a painter, lately arrived here, confirmed the ill news, which I suppose you know, of poor Stewart Abercromby, the Episcopal Minister's son, who was hanged at Edinburgh for having killed a man in warm blood, the quarrel, as I hear, being for the reputation of Stewart's wife, whom he had but lately married. I suppose it went harder with him, he being concerned in the last affair in Scotland for the King I wish he had died then of the wounds received for our Master "

Aberdeen, Alexander, of Cairnbulg, Merchant, Aberdeen

Second son of Andrew Aberdeen, merchant in Aberdeen, made burgess on 8 September 1673 Married Elspet, sister of John Ross of Clochan and Arnage Their eldest son, Alexander, born 1710 was Provost of Aberdeen in 1742

Abernethy, John, of Mayen

Eldest son of Alexander Abernethy, 1st of Mayen, and his wife, Isobel Hacket, whose family had previously owned the estate John married Jean, daughter of James Moir, 2nd of Stoneywood by his first wife, Mary Scroggie, and had two daughters, Jean and Elizabeth, and a son, James, 3rd of Mayen, who married Jane Duff of Hatton, and having shot John Leith of Leithhall in Aberdeen in 1763, was outlawed and fled to France where he was visited by Lord Fife in 1766

Aboyne, John, 3rd Earl of

Son of Charles, 2nd Earl of Aboyne, and his wife, Elizabeth Lyon, second daughter of Patrick, 3rd Earl of Strathmore and Kinghorn

Achmoutie, Captain John

Had a Commission in the French service in 1692, and a MS at Avignon mentions "Le Capitaine Auchmooty, prisonier a Edimbourg 7 Avril 1716".

Achmoutie, Patrick, servant to the Earl Marischal

"He surrendered his arms and accoutrements to Lord Edward Murray, Deputy Liet. of the County of Perth, upon the proclamation but is now a prisoner and is past 60 years of age "

Adie, David, Merchant, Aberdeen

Son of David Adie, styled "of Newark" and Easter Echt, and his wife, Katherine, daughter of David Skene, half-brother of Sir George Skene of Fintray, young David was also great-grandson of George Jamesone, the artist, his grandmother being the latter's daughter.

Ainslie, Patrick

Servant to Mary Duncan, in the Mains of Kildrummy, was one of a party taken near Burntisland by the Dutch when they were fetching coal on 11 January 1716.

Ainslie, William of Blackhill

Alexander, Alexander, Writer in Edinburgh

Alexander, John, Painter

Marjorie Jameson, daughter of George Jameson, "the Socttish Vandyck," married John Alexander, advocate, Edinburgh and John Alexander, the artist born about 1690, was their son.

Alexander, The Rev John, Church of Scotland Minister of Kildrummy

Obtained degree at St Andrews in 1661. Married Anna Gordon and had two daughters and one son, John. He died in August 1717 aged about 76, and was buried in Kildrummy.

Allardyce, John, Merchant and Provost of Aberdeen

Called "John Allardes" in most of the Records. Was Provost of Aberdeen for three terms of two years each, the dates of his election being 1700, 1708 and 1712; the first Parliament of Queen Anne and what proved to be the *last* Scottish Parliament, 1703-1707. Son of John "Allardes," merchant burgess of Aberdeen (died 3 Dec 1699, aged 99), and his wife, Isobel Walker, who died in 1680, aged 83. Married firstly to Agnes Mercer, who died 21 Aug 1700 aged 41 and secondly to Jean Smart, who survived the Provost and died 29 Nov 1722, aged 45,aged 60.

Anderson, Alexander, Aberdeen

Known as "Skipper Anderson", eldest son of Captain John Anderson of Bourtie, who died in 1673. Had five children and died before 1728.

Anderson, Alexander, of Arradoull

Son of James Anderson, sometime of Auchinreath. Said to have married Anne, daughter of Sir John Gordon of Park, by his third wife, Katherine Ogilvie of Kempcairn, and died in 1727, being at that time practically bankrupt.

Arbuthnot, Thomas, of Peterhead and of Rora 1715 & 1745

Born in 1681, eldest son of Nathaniel Arbuthnot in Auchlee, Longside, and Elspet Duncan Married Christian, daughter of William Young, merchant of Peterhead, and had three sons, James, the eldest, born in 1710, and seven daughters. Died 24 March 1762, aged 81.

Arbuthnot, Alexander, Dyer, Peterhead

Brother of Thomas Arbuthnot of Peterhead and of Rora, born in 1687. Married twice, first to Anna, daughter of James Ogilvie of Boyne, and secondly to Mary, daughter of Alexander Scott of Auchtydonald.

Baird, William, of Auchmedden

Son of James Baird, younger of Auchmedden, and his wife, Lady Katherine Hay, daughter of George, 2nd Earl of Kinnoull. This James, who died of smallpox in 1681, was eldest son of Sir James Baird, Knight of Auchmedden, and Christian, only daughter of Sir Walter Ogilvie of Boyne.

Bannerman, Sir Alexander, 2nd Bart. of Elsick
Eldest son of Sir Alexander Bannerman, 1st Baronet of Elsick, created by Charles II in 1682. Married in 1699, Isabella, daughter of Sir Donald Macdonald, 3rd Baronet of Sleat, and by her had one son, Alexander, who succeeded to the title, and three daughters Died in February 1742.

Bannerman, George, brother of Sir Alexander, 2nd Bart.
Son of Sir Alexander, 1st Baronet of Elsick and his wife Margaret, daughter of Patrick Scott of Thirlestane George was at Marischal College with his brother Alexander from 1688-92

Bannerman, Captain John 1715
Described as "Uncle of the Provost," ie Sir Patrick Bannerman Fourth son of Alexander Bannerman of Elsick by his second marriage.

Bannerman, Mark, first cousin of the Provost
Sir Alexander Bannerman, 1st Baronet of Elsick, had a younger half-brother Robert, Episcopal Minister of Newton (Dalkeith) who was deposed for not praying for William and Mary and for refusing to take the Oath in 1689 He married Margaret, daughter of Sir Mark Carse of Cockpen, and the above Mark was his youngest son

Bannerman, Sir Patrick, brother of George and Sir Alexander
Fourth son of Sir Alexander Bannerman, he married Margaret, daughter of Sir Charles Maitland of Pitrichie, by whom he had two sons. Died 4 June 1733

Bisset, James, of Lessendrum
The eldest son of Robert Bisset, 9th of Lessendrum and his wife, Agnes, daughter of Sir Alexander Abercromby, 1st Baronet of Birkenbog Died in 1748

Black, Gilbert, Under-Master at the Grammar School, Aberdeen
Son of Gilbert Black, late Baillie, was at Marischal College from 1680-84.

Black, Dr Robert, Physician to Lord Panmure
Was at battle of Sheriffmuir; escaped from Arbroath on the same vessel with Lord Panmure, on whom he was in close attendance from the time of his rescue, and arrived with him at Avignon on 2 April 1716

Black, William, Regent and Sub-Principal, King's College, Aberdeen
Sometimes described as "of Haddo " His daughter, Elizabeth, married Peter Farquharson of Inverey

Blair, Dr Robert, Physician to Lord Panmure
At the Battle of Sheriffmuir, escaped from Arbroath on the same vessel with Lord Panmure.

Blair, The Rev William, Church of Scotland Minister
Son of Rev Robert Blair, Minister of Alvah Minister at Forglen in 1667, transferred to Fordyce in 1675 He married and had two sons and three daughters. He died in 1716.

Bowman, James, farmer, Aberdeenshire
Captured by the Dutch near Burntisland 11 January 1716.

Brebner, James, Merchant in Aberdeen

Succeeded his father, John Brebner in Cottown, as "heir in Over Corskie in the parish of Kinerney, 9 January 1709."

Brockie, James, Shipmaster, Aberdeen

Met at Mistress Hepburn's house on 22 September (see William Hepburn).

Brodie, George, Servant to Sir James Gordon of Park.

Brown, Andrew, Merchant, Fraserburgh

A warrant had been issued for his arrest, but he was allowed bail on promising he would "carrie himself Loyally to his Majesty King George."

Buchan, Major-General Thomas

Third son of James Buchan of Auchmacoy, who died in 1659, and his wife, Margaret, daughter of Alexander Seton of Pitmedden. Born about 1641.

Buchan, Major James, of Auchmacoy

Nephew of General Thomas Buchan, who had two brothers. Of these, the elder, Alexander, married Mary Ramsay and died leaving an only daughter, when Acuhmacoy passed to the next brother, James. He married Jean Fraser of Tyrie and had two sons, Alexander, a priest who died in 1716 and James, the Major above, the Laird. Married in 1707, Mary, second daughter of Sir John Forbes of Craigievar and widow of John Ramsay of Laithers. By her he had seven sons (Thomas, his heir being born in 1708) and died in 1726.

Burnes, Robert, *grandfather of Robert Burns*

The family originally was called Burnes; it was only because it was pronounced in Ayrshire as if written "Burns" that the Poet and his brother, about 1786, consulted together and agreed to drop Burnes and assume Burns.

Burnett, Andrew, of Eldrick

Second son of Robert Burnett of Elrick, Newmachar, by his first wife, Bessie, daughter of Andrew Burnett of Durris. Married Marjorie in 1707, elder daughter of Sir John Johnston, 4th Baronet of Caskieben, and by her had four sons and four daughters. Died in 1720, aged about 35, and his widow in October 1723.

Burnett, The Rev Andrew, Church of Scotland Minister in Aberdeen

Son of James Burnett, Burgess of Aberdeen. Described by Woodrow as "a very weak, empty volatile man, of no great parts of learning and just made a tool of to disturb the established constitution." He wrote *The Spiritual Anatomy of Man*, published in London, 1693. He married twice (1) Margaret, third daughter of Sir Alexander Burnett of Leys, widow of Alexander Burnett of Monboddo, and had at least five children by her; (2) Elizabeth Reid, widow of Adam Maltman, Merchant, Aberdeen. He died 24 Oct 1716.

Burnett, George, Apothecary

Met at Mistress Hepburn's house on 22 September (see William Hepburn).

Burnett, James, of Monboddo

Only son of Alexander, second of Monboddo, and his wife Margaret, daughter of Sir Alexander Burnett of Leys, 2nd Baronet. Born in 1688, married 3 Nov 1709 Elizabeth, daughter of Sir William Forbes of Craigievar. They had three daughters and eleven sons, amongst whom was the famour Lord Monboddo.

Burnett, John, Merchant, Aberdeen

Nicknamed "Bonnie John," he was son of John Burnett of "Daladies," descended from the family of Leys, and his wife, Agnes, daughter of Turnbull of Strathcathro He married firstly, 15 June 1703, Katherine, second daughter of George Paton of Grandhome; their eldest son John, born 1704, also a merchant in Aberdeen, married Thoeodosia Stuart of Dens and from them are descended the Burnett-Stuarts of Dens and Crichie; secondly, Katherine, third daughter of John Gordon of Fechil, and had a son by her, James Burnett, Merchant in Aberdeen. He survived the Rising

Burnett, Robert, junior, Merchant, Aberdeen 1715

Cornet in the Town's troop of thirty Horse.

Burnett, Thomas, of Kirkhill 1715

Son of Alexander Burnett, 1st of Kirkhill, Dyce   Married with two sons, Thomas and David, and a daughter Agnes. Died in Nov 1763.

Calder, Alexander, younger, of Aswanley (Glass) 1715

Merchant and coppersmith in Old Aberdeen   Married Katherine Forbes of Balfluig and died on 6 Feb 1768, aged 86.

Campbell, The Rev George, Church of Scotland Minister of Alvah

A native of Aberdeenshire, he received his degree at King's College in July 1672. He married on 20 January 1717, Elizabeth Barclay and had two sons, George and Archibald, and a daughter, Elizabeth   He died in Boyndie

Cargill, Thomas, Auchtydonald 1715

Reputed to have been a poet   Married to Anna Abercromby.

Carnegie, John, Dyer, Aberdeen 1715

In St Nicholas Churchyard is a tombstone to· "John Carnegie, Litster in Aberdeen, who dyed 15th April 1735, aged 69. also Elizabeth Carnegie his spouse, who dyed 6th October 1726, aged 55, with James Carnegie, Litster in Abdn their son, who dyed 22nd February 1744, aged 38, and Mary Thomson his spouse who dyed 7 Sept. 1768, aged 60". He was son of James Carnegie, Litster in Aberdeen, who died in 1705, and Jean Ferguson his wife.

Cattanach, George

Met at Mistress Hepburn's house on 22 September (see William Hepburn).

Cattanach, James, Baillie, Aberdeen

One of those who elected the new Jacobite Magistrates of Aberdeen, in the New Church on 29 September 1715.

Cattanach, John, of Bellastraid 1715 & 1745

Sometimes called George   Possibly a Mackintosh by descent. Married first a daughter of Robert Lumsden of Corrachree and secondly Jean Forbes of Belnabodach.

Cattanach, Patrick, in Mickle Mill, Ellon
Prevented Mr James Burnett, who had been Minister at the Presbytery of Ellon, from officiating in his own church on 16 October 1715.

Catto, James, Shipmaster, Fraserburgh
In May 1716 a warrant had been issued for his arrest, but was allowed bail on promising he would "carrie himself Loyally to his Majesty King George under penalty of 500 merks Scots." Perhaps the father of William Catto, Merchant in Aberdeen, at Marischal College in 1719.

Chalmers, Charles, Portlethan
Second son of James Chalmers, Prof of Philosophy at Marischal College. Maried first Jean, daughter of Alexander Boog of Burnhouses, Berwickshire and then Helen, daughter of Alexander Young, Bishop of Liverpool. Was killed at Sheriffmuir, 13 Nov 1715.

Chalmers, The Rev George, Church of Scotland Minister of Botriphnie
Married in 1585, Margaret, daughter of Henry Stewart of Newton of Boharm, and had two sons. He died on 24 Feb 1727 in his 73rd year.

Chalmers, Dr Patrick, Professor of Medicine, Marischal College, Aberdeen
Eldest son of Rev William Chalmers, Minister of Skene. Died about 1727.

Charles, Alexander, Procurator, Aberdeen
Born in 1672. Married 2 Dec 1701, Margaret, only child of James Liddell, mathematic tutor at Marischal College, and by her had four sons and two daughters. Died on 25 March 1754, aged 82.

Clark, Captain, Portsoy
Menioned in Major Fraser's MS.

Clark, Alexander, Shipmaster in Portsoy

Clark, Alexander, Shipmaster, Banff
Born between 1670-1680, was a shipowner in Banff and traded between there and Holland. Before 1709 he married Christian Gordon, and had ten children. Died 8 Oct 1732.

Clark, John, Merchant, Aberdeen
Son of John Clark, merchant in Aberdeen. Married in 1710, Anna, daughter of Walter Cochran of Drumbreck (Provost of Aberdeen 1691-2) and his wife Margaret Butler. Died before 1736.

Collison, Charles, of Auchlunies
Son of Thomas Collison of Auchlunies and his wife, Jean Menzies, and grandson of John Collison, Provost of Aberdeen in 1594. Died in 1749 when the financial affairs of the family were at a low ebb.

Cook, Thomas, farmer, Aberdeenshire
Captured by the Dutch near Burntisland 11 January 1716

Cook, Thomas
Tenant of David Lumsden of Cushnie "forced to be in the Rebellion by the threats and force of the Earl of Mar" and taken prisoner at Preston in November 1715 with 12 other tenants of David Lumsden or Harry Lumsden of Auchindoir and Robert Reid of Mid Clove. Transported from Liverpool to Virginia in 1716.

Cooper, Alexander, Music-Master, Aberdeen

Married in 1705 Margaret, daughter of Alexander Robertson, Town Clerk of Aberdeen, and his first wife Barbara Cruickshank Children named Alexander, John, George, Anna, Issobell and Christian Died in 1722.

Cow, John

Reference in the Jacobite Cess Roll for Aberdeenshire in 1715 "1st February 1716 John Cow was paid £10"

Crichton, James, of Auchingoul

Son of George Crichton of Auchingoul (younger brother of James, 1st Viscount Frendraught) who married, before 1665, Jean, daughter of Sir Alexander Irvine of Drum He died before 16 November 1744 having apparently disinherited the eldest of his four sons.

Cruickshank, George, Merchant and Baillie, Aberdeen

Son of George Cruickshank of Berriehillock, Dean of Guild in Aberdeen, 1664 "George Cruickshank younger, merchant, late Masater of the Kirk-work, and Anna Gordon, his spouse, had a son named Alexander, baptized 9 Jan 1698." Died in 1737

Cruickshank, George

Jacobite at Fraserburgh where the town was searched for the arms left by Lord Lovat and John Forbes of Culloden These were delivered to George Keith, younger of Ludquharn

Cumine, George, of Pitullie

Born in 1695, he was the only son, by his third marriage, of William Cuming of Lochtervandick, Provost of Elgin, who sold Lochtervandich to Alexander Duff of Braco, and bought Auchry and Pitullie Married in 1719 Jean, daughter of Capt Robert Urquhart of Burdsyards, by whom he had four sons and two daughters Jean Urquhart died in 1728, and in 1731 he married his cousin, Christian, daughter of Sir John Guthrie of Ludquharn, and had by her seventeen children' He died on 12 December 1767 at Pittendrum, aged 72

Cumming, John, Merchant, Aberdeen

Taxer appointed by the Town of Aberdeen.

Dalgarno, Mr James, Chamberlain to the Earl Marischal

Jacobite at Fraserburgh where the town was searched for the arms left by Lord Lovat and John Forbes of Culloden These were delivered to George Keith, younger of Ludquharn Son of Rev William Dalgarno and his wife Anna Keith

Davidson, Alexander, of Newton

Eldest son of Alexander Davidson, and his first wife, Jean Burnett. Married on 2 Nov 1701 at Fyvie Church, Mary Gordon of Gight. He had seven children, and Alexander, the son who succeeded took the name of Gordon. He died in 1732.

Davidson, James, of Tillymorgan

Second son of Alexander Davidson of Newton. Died on 17 September 1720, unmarried, his nephew Alexander Davidson Gordon of Gight was served heir in 1735

Davidson, Patrick, Ground Officer at Aboyne

Tenant of the Earl of Aboyne

Davidson, William
Tenant of David Lumsden of Cushnie "forced to be in the Rebellion by the threats and force of the Earl of Mar" and taken prisoner at Preston in November 1715 with 12 other tenants of David Lumsden or Harry Lumsden of Auchindoir and Robert Reid of Mid Clove. Transported from Liverpool to Virginia on the *Friendship* 24 May 1716, landed in Maryland August 1716.

Day, John, Porter, King's College, Aberdeen
Was suspected of being a sympathiser.

Deuchar, Alexander, Merchant, Aberdeen

Donald, James, Banchory-Ternan

Donaldson, John, Writer in Turriff and Banff

Douglas, Rev George, Catholic Priest (also known as Dalgleish)
Son of Colin Douglas and his wife Elizabeth Irvine, born in 1681. He went to the Scots College in Rome in 1698 and returned to Scotland in April 1706. Thought to have been ordained in 1707 in the Highlands by Bishop Gordon, which, if it is true, was the first ordination in the country since the Reformation. He died in Morar on 29 April 1748.

Douglas, John, Marchant, Aberdeen
Son of Sylvester Douglas of Whiteriggs

Douglas, Patrick
Nephew of Sylvester Douglas of Whiteriggs

Douglas, The Rev Robert, Minister of Bothwell
Younger son of the Rev Robert Douglas, Bishop of Dunblane, brother to Sylvester Douglas of Whiteriggs.

Douglas, Sylvester, of Whiteriggs
Eldest son of Robert Douglas, Bishop of Dunblane. Married Margaret, daughter of Major George Keith of Whiteriggs, and thus obtained the estate in 1703.

Douglas, William
Nephew of Sylvester Douglas of Whiteriggs.

Duff, Alexander, of Drummuir
First cousin of William Duff, eldest son of Provost William Duff of Inverness and his first wife, Christian, daughter of Alexander Duff of Kinloss. Born in 1657 and married in 1684, Katherine, orphan daughter of Adam Duff, bankrupt Laird of Drummuir. By her he had eleven children, amongst them a daughter Anne, born 1684, who married Lachlan Mackintosh. Died in 1726.

Duff, John, Messenger, Aberdeen
Son of John Duff of Aberdeen of the Muldavit family and his wife Margaret Johnstone. Reported to have died in Rotterdam in 1718, but also that he was drowned returning with Taylor of Boyndie in 1718 and both their bodies got clasped with a rope and an oak plank. "Boyndie, in life, got on the shore of Musselburgh, retained the black mark of the log on his head, but Duff drowned."

Duff, William, of Dipple
Uncle of successor of William Duff of Braco, was second son of Alexander Duff of Keithmore and Helen Grant of Allachie. He married

twice, first, Jean Gordon of Edinglassie, and secondly, Jean Dunbar of Durn. By his first wife he was the father of William, Lord Braco, afterwards first Lord Fife. He had three other sons who died young, and ten daughters, of whom the eldest, Helen, married the Hon William Sutherland. Two younger daughters were named Anne and Janet.

Duff, William, of Inverness
Father of Alexander Duff of Drummuir, and third son of Adam Duff of Clunybeg. Born in 1632. Died before end 1715.

Duguid, Alexander, Auchinhove, brother of Robert Duguid
Lieutenant under Glenbucket's command. Nephew to Dr Patrick Abercromby.

Duguid, Patrick Leslie, younger of Auchinhove 1715 & 1745
Son of Robert Duguid of Auchinhove, born in 1700, educated abroad and returned from Douai just before Rising of 1715. He married in 1730 Isabella Dickson, by whom he had three sons and one daughter, all dying in infancy. He married secondly, in 1740, Amelia, daughter of John Irvine of Kingcausie, by whom he had eleven children, the fourth son, John, ultimately succeeding him. Patrick Leslie Duguid's second wife having died in 1762, he married for the third time, in 1773, his cousin Eliza, sister of Patrick Leslie Grant. Died at the house of Tullos on 11 April 1777.

Duguid, Robert, of Auchinhove
9th Laird of Auchinhove and eldest son of Francis Duguid, 8th of Auchinhove and his wife, Marie Abercromby. Francis died in 1698 and in 1699 Robert married Teresa Leslie, third daughter of Patrick, Count Leslie of Balquhain. By her he had a family of four sons, the eldest being Patrick Leslie Duguid, his heir, and two daughters. Died in 1731.

Duguid, Patrick Leslie, younger of Auchinhove
Dunbar, Sir James, of Durn
Eldest son of Sir William Dunbar, 1st Baronet of Durn, and his wife Janet, daughter of John Brodie, Dean of Auldearn. Baptized on 9 January 1665; he married in 1692, Mary (or Margaret) daughter of James Baird, younger of Auchmedden, and by her had two sons, William, who succeeded him and James of Kincorth. Died in November 1737, his wife having predeceased him in 1734.

Dunbar, Jerome
Tenant of David Lumsden of Cushnie "forced to be in the Rebellion by the threats and force of the Earl of Mar" and taken prisoner at Preston in November 1715 with 12 other tenants of David Lumsden or Harry Lumsden of Auchindoir and Robert Reid of Mid Clove. Some were transported to Virginia. Jerome Dunbar returned from there.

Dunbar, The Rev William, Church of Scotland Minister of Cruden
Made Bishop in 1727 and in 1731 was recognised as Bishop of Moray and Ross. He died in 1746, aged 85.

Dunbreck (or Dumbreck), The Rev Patrick, Episcopalian Clergyman
Dunn (or Deune), attending Aberdeen University classes in 1680.
Dunn, James, Merchant in Aberdeen

Erroll, Charles, 13th Earl of
Eldest son of Sir John Hay, 12th Earl of Erroll, and Lady Anne Drummond, only daughter of James, 3rd Earl of Perth. Between 1712-15 lived on the Continent. Died, unmarried, 16 October 1717 aged 40, when the title devolved on his elder sister, Mary, Countess of Erroll. He had another sister Margaret.

Erskine, James
Uncle to the Laird of Pittodrie. Younger son of Thomas Erskine of Pittodrie who in 1643 married Helen, daughter of Sir William Auchinleck of Balmanno. Married a Mowat "heiress of Balquholly".

Erskine, Thomas, of Pittodrie
Eldest son of William Erskine, 6th of Pittodrie and his wife Mary, daughter of Patrick Grant of Ballindalloch. Married twice, in 1705 to Margaret, daughter of Sir Alexander Burnett of Craigmyle, by whom he had a son William, who, being weak in mind, was excluded from the succession to Pittodrie, and secondly on 30 November 1746 the Hon Anne Forbes, daughter of James, 16th Lord Forbes. By her he had an only daughter, Mary, his successor. Died on 14 October 1761 "at a very advanced age"   Anne Forbes died at Pittodrie in November 1750, aged only twenty-seven.

Erskine, William
Brother to Thomas Erskine of Pittodrie. Died in Feb 1774, aged 86.

Ewan, George
Brother of John Ewan, tenant of the Earl of Aboyne.

Ewan, John
Tenant of the Earl of Aboyne.

Ewan, William, in Greencoats
Son of John Ewan, tenant of the Earl of Aboyne.

Farquharson, Alexander (or Alistair), younger of Auchindryne
Eldest son of Lewis Auchindryne. Married in 1721 Claudia, youngest daughter of Charles Innes of Drumgask. Had two sons and two daughters, the elder son Alexander succeeding to Auchindryne and Inverey.

Farquharson, Charles, Inverey
Second son of John Farquharson. Writer to the Signet in 1708. Died, unmarried, in 1747, succeeded by his half-brother James of Balmoral.

Farquharson, Charles, of Balmoral
Eldest son of William Farquharson of Inverey and his second wife, Agnes (or Anna), daughter of Alexander Gordon of Abergeldie. Half-brother to John Farquharson. Died unmarried before November 1718.

Farquharson, Charles, Whitehouse
Second son of Harry Farquharson of Whitehouse. Married daughter of Grant of Garthenmore and had two daughters.

Farquharson, Daniel, Merchant in Aberdeen
Taxer appointed by the Town of Aberdeen.

Farquharson, Donald, of Micras

Younger of two sons of Alexander Farquharson, 3rd of Allanquoich by Jean Forbes of Skellater. Maried firstly Murrel Gordon, daughter of Tirriesoul and secondly in 1726 Jean, daughter of James Grant of Gellovie and Knockando.

Farquharson, Donald, of Coldrach

Eldest son of George Farquharson of Coldrach and his wife, Margaret Farquharson, daughter of Allanquoich. Alive still in 1733. By his first wife, Grizel Small of Diranean, he had two sons, George and William.

Farquharson, Francis, younger of Whitehouse

Eldest son of Harry Farquharson of Whitehouse and his first wife Barbara Ross of Auchlossan. Married his cousin, Euphemia Ross of Auchlossan, and died in 1733.

Farquharson, George, younger of Coldrach

Son of Donald Farquharson of Coldrach and his first wife Grizel Small. Married Marjory (or Mary), duaghter of John Farquharson of Inverey and had five children, but only two sons, James and Donald and one daughter were alive in 1733. George died before that year. The elder son, James, who was served heir to his grandfather Donald, in 1751 married Mary Lumsden.

Farquharson, Harry, of Whitehouse

The third Farquharson Laird, he was the only son by the second marriage of James Farquharson WS. He married Barbara Ross of Auchlossan and had Francis and two other children. He married secondly, Elspet Harper, who had been his servant, and by her had Harry of Whitehouse-Mill, who was killed at Culloden.

Farquharson, Harry, of Cults

Son of Arthur Farquharson of Cults (Glengairn).

Farquharson, James, of Balmoral

Half-brother to the Charles and Peter Farquharson. Youngest son by the second marriage of John Farquharson of Inverey and his wife Marjory, daughter of George Leith of Overhall. Married Jane, daughter of William Leith of the Overhall family, but had no children. Merchant in Aberdeen. Died about 1753.

Farquharson, John, of Kirkton of Aboyne

Son of Thomas, son of John, third son of Finlay Farquharson, who was second son of Robert Farquharson, 1st of Invercauld. Married twice, first to Helen, daughter of Dr William Muir, Archdeacon of St Andrews and secondly to a daughter of Dr Alexander Pennycuick of Newhall of Ramanno.

Farquharson, John, Auchindryne

Second son of Lewis Farquharson. Born 15 April 1699. Died 22 August 1782 at Balmoral.

Farquharson, John, Whitehouse

Third and youngest son of Harry Farquharson of Whitehouse. Married and had three daughters. Described as "a surgeon in London".

Farquharson, Lawrence, in Cobletown of Tullich

Son of Donald Farquharson in Cobletown of Tullich, eldest son of Donald Farquharson, 2nd of Allanquoich by his second wife, Helen Garden. Transported from Liverpool to the West Indies, where he lived and died.

Farquharson, Lewis, of Auchindryne

Eldest son of James Farquharson, 1st of Inverey, and his second wife, Agnes Ferris. Entered a contract of marriage on 18 December 1693, with his cousin Margaret, second daughter of Alexander Farquharson of Allanaquoich, by whom he had six sons, Alexander, John, William, Donald, Charles and James. He also had three daughters. Died before 30 Nov 1729.

Farquharson, Peter, of Inverey

Eldest son of John Farquharson, 3rd of Inverey and his first wife, Margaret Gordon. Peter, sometimes called Patrick, married twice, first to Margaret, daughter of Thomas Nairn, Kirkhill, Perthshire by whom he had three daughters, and secondly to Elizabeth, daughter of William Black, Sub-Principal of King's College, Aberdeen, by whom he had three sons and two daughters. Died in 1737, succeeded by his son Joseph, afterwards by his son Benjamin. His widow survived him till 1766.

Farquharson, Peter, of the Whitehouse family

Grandson of James Farquharson, 1st of Whitehouse. Died in 1715 after an unsuccessful leg amputation.

Farquharson, Robert, of Allanquoich

Uncle of Lawrence in Cobletown of Tullich. Second son of Donald, 2nd of Allanquoich, and Helen Garden, daughter of Bellamore. Married Mary, daughter of Peter Gordon of Minmore, but left only a natural son.

Farquharson, Shaw, of the Achriachan family

Sixth son of Gregor Farquharson of Wester Camdell, who married Mary, daughter of John Mackenzie of Dalmore. Shaw was killed at Sheriffmuir.

Farquharson, Thomas, Merchant, Aberdeen

Taxer appointed by the Town of Aberdeen.

Ferguson, Francis

Tenant of David Lumsden of Cushnie "forced to be in the Rebellion by the threats and force of the Earl of Mar" and taken prisoner at Preston in November 1715 with 12 other tenants of David Lumsden or Harry Lumsden of Auchindoir and Robert Reid of Mid Clove. Transported from Liverpool to Antigua on the *Scipio* on 30 Mar 1716.

Ferries, George, farmer in Strathdon

Captured by the Dutch near Burntisland 11 January 1716.

Findlater, George, Excise Officer, Peterhead

Helped to break open the Clerk's room in Fraserburgh "with ane bigg hammer" and removed the "24 firelocks charged with powder and balls."

13

Findlater, John, Master of the Grammar School, Aberdeen

Son of Alexander Findlater, burgess of Aberdeen, born 1652. Died on 16 November 1717 aged 75, buried in St Nicholas Churchyard with his "beloved wives" Christian Burnet and Elizabeth Donaldson, and four children.

Finnie, John

Tenant of David Lumsden of Cushnie "forced to be in the Rebellion by the threats and force of the Earl of Mar" and taken prisoner at Preston in November 1715 with 12 other tenants of David Lumsden or Harry Lumsden of Auchindoir and Robert Reid of Mid Clove. Transported from Liverpool to Virginia 1716.

Fraser, Patrick, Catholic Priest

Forbes, Alexander, "youngest," Merchant in Aberdeen

Taxer appointed by the Town of Aberdeen.

Forbes, Alexander, younger of Balfluig

A younger son of John Forbes of Balfluig. Baptized on 8 May 1699.

Forbes, Alexander, Lord Pisligo

Born 1678. Escaped to Italy. Died 1762.

Forbes, Alexander, of Lockermick, Merchant, Aberdeen

The son of William Forbes in Lockermick, born in 1673. Married Janet Gordon and had at least one son, George. He died on 24 April 1738. His widow survived him.

Forbes, Alexander

Jacobite at Fraserburgh where the town was searched for the arms left by Lord Lovat and John Forbes of Culloden. These were delivered to George Keith, younger of Ludquham.

Forbes, The Hon Archibald

Born on 3 November 1697, third son of William, 13th Lord Forbes and his wife Anne, daughter of James Brodie of Brodie.

Forbes, Arthur, Echt, Merchant, Aberdeen

Taxer appointed by the Town of Aberdeen. At Marischal College, Aberdeen, from 1700 to 1704.

Forbes, Charles, Brux

Sixth son of Arthur Forbes, 10th of Brux and his wife Elizabeth Murray. Married and had a son, Captain Roderick, whoo died in Persia in 1760.

Forbes, Charles, Merchant, Aberdeen

Possibly younger brother of John Forbes of Upper Boyndlie, the Collector of Cess.

Forbes, George, of Culquhanny

Fourth son of Arthur Forbes of Culquhanny, born in 1687. Married 11 June 1708 to Elizabeth Gordon of Acuhindoir. His widow remarried in 1720.

Forbes, George, 4th of Skellater

Eldest son of George Forbes, 3rd of Skellater. Married twice, first in 1714 to Christian, daughter of John Forbes of Inverernan and secondly, Isobel, daughgter of John Gordon of Blelack. He died in 1730 and was succeeded by his son, George.

Forbes, The Hon James
Second son of William, 13th Lord Forbes. He was born in 1689 and married twice, first in 1715 to Mary, daughter of Alexander, 3rd Lord Forbes of Pitsligo and widow of John Forbes, younger of Monymusk, by whom he had one son, James, and three daughters, and secondly, in August 1741, Elizabeth, daughter of Sir James Gordon, Bart. of Park, Banffshire, by whom he had no issue. He died in 1761.

Forbes, John, of Invererman
The famous "Black Jock", he was born in 1666 or 1664, and married in 1684. Fifth son of William Forbes, 2nd of Skellater and only son of his second wife, Agnes, daughter of William McIntosh of Kyllachy and widow of Alexander McGillivray, younger of Drumnaglass. He married twice, first in 1684 to Elspet Stewart, by whom he had nine sons, and two daughters. His second wife, whom he married in 1709 was Margaret, daughter of the Rev Thomas Alexander, Minister of Logie Coldstone and had two sons by her. He died of wounds in 1716, a prisoner in Carlisle, a day before he was due to be hanged.

Forbes, John, of Belnabodach
Son of William Forbes and his wife Mary Stewart of Lesmurdie. He married on 7 November 1706, Janet, daughter of John Robertson, Minister of Invernochty.

Forbes, John, of Invernettie
Son of William Forbes of Ledinglassie, sometimes called "of Invernettie," who was brother of George, 3rd of Skellater. Married Rebecca (sometimes called Rachel) youngest daughter of John Forbes of Ledmacoy, and had at least one son, William. Shot in 1715 or 1716 by some dragoons commanded by Lord Forbes.

Forbes, John, of Upper Boyndlie
Fourth son of Sir John Forbes, 3rd of Monymusk, and his second wife Barbara, daughter of Sir John Dalmahoy, Bart. Born at Monymusk in 1680, he married on 27 April 1704 Susanna (born 1680) second daughter of George Morison of Bognie and Frendraught and had five sons and six daughters. Drowned November 1716.

Forbes, John, younger of Waterton
Eldest son of Thomas Forbes of Waterton and his first wife, Elizabeth Nicolson, second daughter of Sir George Nicholson of Balcaskie. Killed at Sheriffmuir.

Forbes, Lachlan, of Edinglassie
Fourth son of George Forbes, 3rd of Skellater, born in 1677. He married Margaret, daughter of Robert Irvine, Minister of Towie. He had at least one son, Benjamin.

Forbes, Nathaniel, of Ardgeith
Second son of George Forbes, 3rd of Skellater. Married with many children.

Forbes, Thomas, of Tolquhon family
Second son of Thomas Forbes of Little Auchry and his wife Henrietta, daughter of James Erskine, Lord Auchterhouse, he was born in 1689.

Forbes, Thomas
    Tenant of David Lumsden of Cushnie "forced to be in the Rebellion by the threats and force of the Earl of Mar" and taken prisoner at Preston in November 1715 with 12 other tenants of David Lumsden or Harry Lumsden of Auchindoir and Robert Reid of Mid Clove. Transported from Liverpool to Virginia on the *Friendship* 24 May 1716, landed in Maryland Aug 1716, returned to Scotland 1722.

Forbes, Thomas of Tolquhon
    Born 1689 son of Thomas Forbes of Little Auchry and Henrietta Erskine. Fled via London to France Sept 1716, died London 1728.

Forbes, William of Ellon

Forbes, William, of Blackton
    Born 28 Nov 1699, son of Alexander Forbes of Blackton (King Edward) and his wife, Isobel Hacket, widow of Alexander Abernethy of Mayen. Born on 28 November 1689, he married twice, first on 31 Aug 1714 to Janet, sister of Joseph Brodie of Muiresk and had one daughter Isabel; secondly in 1722 Ann, daughter of Thomas Forbes of Gavell, by whom he had one son who died before his father. Died on 9 Oct 1771.

Forbes, William, younger of Invernettie
    Son of John Forbes, 3rd of Invernettie and his wife Rebecca Forbes of Ledmacoy. Born in 1694.

Forbes, William, of Tombeg
    Son of John Forbes (of the Monymusk family) and Anna Lunan, daughter of the Minister of Monymusk. Born in 1687, he married Anna, daughter of Alexander Forbes, Minister of Fintray.

Forbes, William, Echt, Merchant, Aberdeen
    Taxer appointed by the Town of Aberdeen. At Marischal College, Aberdeen, from 1700 to 1704.

Fraser, Lord Charles, of Muchals
    Fourth and last Lord Fraser, only son of Andrew, 3rd Lord Fraser and his first wife, Katherine, daughter of the 7th Lord Lovat, widow of Viscount Arbuthnot and before that of Sir John Sinclair of Dunbeath. Born in Sept 1662, in Sept 1683 he married Mary or Marjorie Erskine, daughter of James, 7th Earl of Buchan and widow of Simon Fraser of Inverallochy. He died by falling from a cliff at Pennan on 12 October 1716.

Fraser, The Hon James, of Lonmay
    Third son of William, 11th Lord Saltoun and his wife Margaret, daughter of James Sharpe, Archbishop of St Andrews. Married in 1726 Lady Eleanor Lindsay,m daughter of Colin, 3rd Earl of Balcarres, and had one son, William, who died abroad. Died on 10 Aug 1729; his widow surviving him for six years.

Fraser, Captain Simon
    Cousin to William Fraser of Inverallochy, he was son of a younger brother of the Simon of Inverallochy, who married Lady Marjorie Erskine.

Fraser, William, of Inverallochy

Stepsun of Lord Charles of Muchals.   Second son of Simon Fraser of Inverallochy and his wife Lady Marjorie Erskine, daughter of the Earl of Buchan.   Killed at Sheriffmuir.

Fullarton, James, Advocate, Aberdeen

Third son of Robert Udny of Auchterellon and Elizabeth, only daughter of Col John Fullarton of Dudwick, James assumed the name of Fullarton.   Married Jean Walker and had six sons and five daughters.   He is supposed to have died in 1761.

Fullarton, John, of Dudwick

Brother of James Fullarton, second son of Robert Udny of Auchterellon, he took the name of Fullarton when he succeeded his maternal grandfather in Dudwick in 1689.   Married Mary, duaghter of Sir David Falconer of Newton, and had two sons and three daughters.

Fyfe, James, Baillie and Merchant, Aberdeen

Eldest son of John Fyfe, merchant in Aberdeen, and Elizabeth Tulloch his wife.   He died 13 August 1729.

Garden, Charles, of Bellastrem

Garden, The Rev George, DD, Minister of St Nicholas Church, Aberdeen

Son of Rev Alexander Garden, Minister of Forgue, born in 1648.   He escaped from captivity in Winton's House in the Canongate by changing clothes with his sister.   He died 31 January 1733 in his 85th year, and was buried at Old Machar.

Garden, The Rev James, DD, Professor of Divinity in King's College, Aberdeen

Elder brother of Dr George Garden, born at Forgue in 1646, he graduated at Aberdeen in 1662.   In 1696 he was living in Aberdeen with his wife and nine children.   He died in 1726, aged about 80.

Gatt, The Rev James, Minister of Gretna

A native of Cullen, Banffshire, in 1714 he entered King's College, Aberdeen.   Expelled for forcing the drummer of Old Aberdeen to make a proclamation in February 1716 desiring all persons to come and see the Duke of Brunswick burnt in effigy.   He married Jean, daughter of the Rev James Gowanlock, Minister of Kikpatrick-Fleming, and died 31 Oct 1787, in his 88th year.

Gellie, James, Merchant, Aberdeen

Married 8 April 1714 Elizabeth, eldest daughter of Alexander Thomson, Advocate and had at least two sons and a daughter.   Died before 1744.

Gellie, Patrick, Merchant, Aberdeen

Taxer appointed by the Town of Aberdeen.   Son of Patrick Gellie, merchant and burgess of Aberdeen.   Owned Balgarse in Foveran.   He is believed to have died before 1743.

Gordon, Adam, of Balgowan

Second son of William Gordon of Balgowan, Keig, and his wife Isobel Leith.

Gordon, Alexander, Merchant, Aberdeen

Married to Isobel, daughter of James Gordon, Dean of Guild, in 1710, and had five children.

Gordon, Alexander, of Blelack
Second son of John Gordon of Blelack, succeeding to title. Married firstly to Barbara Stewart and secondly to Isobel Forbes, who was described as "a masculine character," and had two sons, John and Charles. He died in 1723.

Gordon, Alexander, of Cairnfeld
Son of Robert Gordon, 6th of Cairnfield.   Later a merchant in Amsterdam.

Gordon, Alexander, Commissary Clerk Depute, Aberdeen
Second son of John Gordon, 2nd of Seaton and Elizabeth Irvine, his wife.   Born in 1688, he married Marjory, daughter of James Milne of Blairton and had three sons and two daughters. He died in 1727.

Gordon, Alexander, in Comrie
Married Jane, and had a son and a daughter before 1696.

Gordon, Alexander, brother of Glenbucket
Son of John Gordon of Knockespock.

Gordon, Alexander, of Glengerack
Son of Charles Gordon of Glengerack and Margaret Duff, eldest daughter of Alexander Duff of Braco.   Born in 1698, he married in 1721 at Inchdrewer Castle, Helen Lauder, daughter of Sir John Lauder, 2nd Baronet of Fountainhall and widow of George, 4th Lord Banff.

Gordon, Alexander, Scurdargue
Was at Sheriffmuir.

Gordon, Alexander
Tenant of David Lumsden of Cushnie "forced to be in the Rebellion by the threats and force of the Earl of Mar" and taken prisoner at Preston in November 1715 with 12 other tenants of David Lumsden or Harry Lumsden of Auchindoir and Robert Reid of Mid Clove.   Transported from Liverpool to Virginia on the *Friendship* 24 May 1716, landed in Maryland Aug 1716.

Gordon, Dr Alexander, Catholic Priest
Captured with Francis Gordon of Craig at Dunfermline on 24 October 1716.   Probably son of Patrick of Glastirem and uncle of James of Glastirem.   Although too ill to march to Carlisle, he survived the rising and retired to Auchindour and died there at an advanced age in 1763.

Gordon, Charles, of Abergeldie
Son of Gordon of Minmore.   Married Rachel, daughter of Alexander Gordon, 8th Laird and Euphemia Graham of Morphie.   They had three sons, Peter, Alexander and Joseph.

Gordon, Charles, of Buthlaw, Advocate, Aberdeen
Son of William Gordon of Buthlaw and his wife Elizabeth, daughter of Captain Robert Martin of Clerkhill, near Peterhead.   Married Jean, daughter of John Udny of Cultercullen and part of Newtyle and by her had six sons and seven daughters.   He died 23 Dec 1751 at a very advanced age.

Facies Civitatis ABERDONIE Veter

Prospect of Old ABERDIEN.

Gordon, Charles, of Tilphoudie
Eldest son of John Gordon, 8th of Tilphoudie by his second wife Elizabeth Duguid of Auchinhove, said to have been killed at Sheriffmuir.

Gordon, Francis, of Craig, 7th Laird
Eldest son of Francis, 6th Laird of Craig, and his first wife, Elizabeth, daughter of Sir Gilbert Menzies of Pitfodels. Born about 1653, he died of wounds in September 1716 at Stirling. He had married Agnes Ogilvie, eldest daughter of George, 2nd Lord Banff and had three sons and five daughters. His second wife was Anna, daughter of William Gordon of Corrachree.

Gordon, Francis, younger of Craig
Eldest son of 7th Laird. Born about 1680 and died in 1727 in England. Married three times, firstly to Elizabeth Barclay of Towie, widow of John Gordon of Rothiemay - no issue; secondly Agnes Forbes of Balfluig, mother of John, 9th Laird of Criag; and thirdly Catherine Campbell of Lundie, widow of Patrick Russell of Moncoffer, with issue, Francis and William.

Gordon, George, of Buckie
Twice married, first about 1706 to Jean Burnett by whom he had a son, George and a daughter, Katherine; secondly in 1717 to Margaret, daughter of George Gordon of Glasterim, and had two sons and four daughters. He died in 1729.

Gordon, George, of Carnousie
Second son of Sir George Gordon of Edinglassie and his second wife, Jean Forbes. Married Jean, daughter of Arthur Forbes of Brux, and had four sons, including Arthur, younger of Carnousie, and four daughters.

Gordon, George, of Dorlaithers
Second son of Alexander Gordon of Auchintoul, Lord Auchintoul and his wife, Isobel Gray, daughter of Gray of Braik. He married Barbara, daughter of Alexander Mackenzie of Artloch, and by her had three sons, and one daughter. Perished at sea escaping to Holland.

Gordon, George, of Glastirem
Second son of Patrick Gordon of Glastirem, married Violet, daughter of Michael Strachan of Auchnagatt. He died in 1721.

Gordon, George, of Kincardine Mill
Son of John, and married to Agnes Gordon, he died before 1720.

Gordon, George, of Sauchen

Gordon, Harry, of Avochie
Eldest son of John Gordon of Avochie. His mother was Isobel Farquharson and his wife was Elizabeth, sister to John Gordon of Glenbucket. They had a son, John.

Gordon, James, of Barnes
Son of George, 1st of Shellagreen, he married Marjorie, one of the eight daughters of John Moir of Barnes and Mary Cochrane; the issue of the marriage being seven daughters but apparently no son. He died before 1739.

Gordon, James, of Ellon

Son of Alexander Gordon, farmer in Bourtie.   He married Elizabeth Livingstone and had five sons and six daughters. He died in 27 Feb 1732.

Gordon, Dr James, of Hilton

Son of Dr John Gordon of Collieston.   Married in 1731 Barbara, daughter of Robert Cuming of Birnes, by whom he had a son John. He died in 1755.

Gordon, James, of Letterfourie

Son of John Gordon of Letterfourie and his first wife, Janet Seton. Married in 1695, Glicerie, daughter of Sir James Dunbar, 2nd Baronet of Durn and had four sons and three daughters.   He died in 1748, aged 88.

Gordon, James, younger of Auchlyne

Second son of James, 2nd of Auchlyne and his wife, Rachel Burnett, the younger James is also called "of Tillyfour".   He married Ann, second daughter of James Sandilands and had one son, James, another son and three daughters.   Killed in 1715, presumably at Sheriffmuir.

Gordon, James, Brewer, Aberdeen

Caputred at Dunfermline 24 Oct 1715 and marched to Edinburgh and then Carlisle 4 Sep 1716 where he was discharged

Gordon, James, Dean of Guild, Aberdeen

Married to Janet Paton, had a son, George, baptized on 21 Jul 1706, and on 27 April 1710 had a daughter, Isobel.   He was buried on 31 Jan 1728, and Jean Strachan, spouse was buried with him on 5 Mar 1728.

Gordon, James, of Balgowan

Son of Adam, of Balgowan.

Gordon, James, of Park

Son of Sir John Gordon, 1st Baronet of Park and his fourth wife, Helen Ogilvy, daughter of James, 2nd Earl of Airlie.   Married twice, firstly in 1709 to Helen Fraser, daughter of William, 11th Lord Saltoun and by her had William, John and Helen, and secondly about 1720, Margaret Elphinstone, daughter of John, 8th Lord Elphinstone and widow of George Leslie of Balquhain, who died in 1715.   By this second marriage he had one son, James Gordon of Cobairdy and three daughters.   Died 15 Dec 1727 of apoplexy.

Gordon, Rev James, Glastirem, Catholic Priest

Son of Patrick Gordon of Glastirem and brother of George Gordon of Glastirem, the family being cadets of Letterfourie.   Born in 1664, was sent to the Scots College in Paris in 1680.   He died in 1746 at Thornhill, near Drummond Castle.

Gordon, John, of Achanacy

A prisoner in Banff in November 1716.

Gordon, John, of Achindachy

Eldest son of Alexander Gordon, 3rd of Auchindachy, who died about 1713, and his wife Katherine Martin. In 1714 he married Jean, eldest daughter of George Innes of Dunkinty, Provost of Elgin, and they had a son, Alexander, and one daughter. There exists a testament of how he beat his wife, who on a number of occasions was only saved by the intervention of others. The House of Auchindachy was described as "ruinous" in 1742. Probably died in 1749. What became of his son is not known.

Gordon, John, of Coldstone
Buried at Lancaster between January and July 1716.

Gordon, Dr John, of Collieston
Son of another Dr John Gordon of Collieston and his first wife, Katherine Fullarton. Married Margaret Dowell and had nine sons, amongst whom was Dr James of Hilton, and several daughters. He died in 1735.

Gordon, John, Cromar
Son of a tenant in Cromar. He refused to serve and was taken prisoner by the Jacobites.

Gordon, John, of Dunmeath
Son of Patrick Gordon of Dunmeath, Banff.

Gordon, John, younger of Lesmoir
Fourth son of Sir James Gordon, 4th Baronet of Lesmoir by his wife, Jane, only daughter of Sir John Gordon of Haddo. Later married Henrietta, daughter of 11th Lord Saltoun by whom he had four sons and six daughters.

Gordon, Dr John, of Seaton, Civilist, King's College
Eldest son of James Gordon, 1st of Seaton, Commissary Clerk, and Marjorie, daughter of Robert Forbes of Rubislaw. Married Elizabeth, only daughter of Richard Irvine of Cairnfield, and had two sons, Richard and Alexander and three daughters. Buried on 28 September 1741.

Gordon, The Rev Ludovick, Minister of Kinoir
Son of the Rev James Gordon, Minister of Rothiemay and his wife, Katharine, and became Laird of Kinmundy. Married to Anna Gordon, he had Alexander and Jean.

Gordon, Patrick, of Auchleuchries
Third son of John Gordon of Auchleuchries and his wife, Elizabeth, daughter of William Grant of Crichie.

Gordon, Patrick, Bogs, North Rhynie

Gordon, Patrick
Tenant of the Earl of Aboyne.

Gordon, Peter, in Drumbulg

Gordon, Richard, Regent of King's College, Aberdeen
Eldest son of John Gordon of Seaton, Civilist, Richard was born in 1687. Married first in 1730 Elizabeth, daughter of John Leith of Leith Hall, with two daughters and secondly, Mary Auchindachy, by whom he had one son, John, and two daughters. Died 9 November 1763, aged 77.

Gordon, Robert, of Cluny
Son of Robert Gordon of Cluny, Advocate. Married with a son, Robert, who served heir to him in Cluny in 1723.

Gordon, Robert, of Hallhead

Son of Patrick Gordon, 9th Laird of Hallhead. Successful wine merchant in Bordeaux. Married Isabel Byres of Tonley and his son was George of the '45. Died in 1738.

Gordon, Robert, younger of Lesmoir

Fifth son of Sir James Gordon.

Gordon, Robert, Scurdargue

Brother of Alexander Gordon of Scurdargue. Fought at Sheriffmuir. He married his own near relative, Elizabeth Gordon of Tolophin, and had children, among them Alexander (1724-1807).

Gordon, William, of Craigwillie

Gordon, William, of Goval

Second son of James Gordon, 1st of Seaton. Married Christian Wyllie and then, before 1710, Elizabeth, daughter of Robert Cruickshank of Banchory, widow of John Johnston, Provost of Aberdeen in 1697. Had sons William and Nathaniel. Died in 1733.

Gordon, William, Merchant, Kintore

May have been a relative of Captain James Gordon, son of Patrick, 1st of Badenscoth, because he witnessed the baptism of Isobel, his daughter, on 23 Oct 1702.

Gordon, William, 3rd of Farskane

Grandson of William, 1st of Farskane, and son of William, 2nd Laird and Helen, second daughter of Alexander Duff of Braco, married before 1700. Married Margaret, daughter of James Duff of Crombie in 1725. Probably died in Norway where he was a merchant.

Grant, Robert

Tenant of David Lumsden of Cushnie "forced to be in the Rebellion by the threats and force of the Earl of Mar" and taken prisoner at Preston in November 1715 with 12 other tenants of David Lumsden or Harry Lumsden of Auchindoir and Robert Reid of Mid Clove. Transported from Liverpool to Maryland on *Godspeed* on 28 Jul 1716, landed in Maryland Oct 1716.

Grant, William

Tenant of David Lumsden of Cushnie "forced to be in the Rebellion by the threats and force of the Earl of Mar" and taken prisoner at Preston in November 1715 with 12 other tenants of David Lumsden or Harry Lumsden of Auchindoir and Robert Reid of Mid Clove. Transported from Liverpool to Virginia on the *Friendship* 24 May 1716, landed in Maryland Aug 1716.

Gray, The Rev Alexander, Minister, Footdee

Son of Thomas Gray, Provost of Aberdeen, born about 1660. Burgess of Aberdeen 1695.

Gray, John, Baillie, Fraserburgh

A warrant had been issued for his arrest, but he was allowed bail on promising he would "carrie himself Loyally to his Majesty King George."

Gray, Patrick

Convenor of the Trades of Aberdeen, died 1736.

Gray, Patrick, Convener of the Trades, Aberdeen
Died before 13 Nov 1736.

Gray, William, farmer, Aberdeenshire
Captured by the Dutch near Burntisland 11 January 1716.

Gray, William
Tenant of David Lumsden of Cushnie "forced to be in the Rebellion by the threats and force of the Earl of Mar" and taken prisoner at Preston in November 1715 with 12 other tenants of David Lumsden or Harry Lumsden of Auchindoir and Robert Reid of Mid Clove. Some were transported to Virginia.

Halket, George
Schoolmaster at Rathen in 1714, deprived in 1723, died at Memsie 1756 and was buried in Fraserburgh. Married in March 1718, Janet Adamson, daughter of Marion Crawford in Rathen, and had three children.

Hamilton, John, Janitor, King's College, Aberdeen
Discharged from his post on 1 May 1716.

Hamilton, John, of Gibston (1715 and 1745)
Tenant of the Duke of Gordon. Married to Janet Mitchell. From Newgate he was hanged on Kennington Common on Nov 1746. He had a son, also named John who succeeded him as Factor to the Duke of Gordon.

Harper, The Rev Adam, Minister of Boharm
Eldest son of the Rev William Harper, Minister of Boharm, and his wife, Elizabeth, daughter of Walter Innes of Auchlunkart. He married twice: (1) 2 Oct 1687, Janet, daughter of Alexander Leslie of Kininvie, by whom he had four sons and three daughters; (2) 31 August 1703, Margaret, daughter of Alexander Gordon of Arradoul, and by her had three sons and six daughters. He died 14 May 1726, aged about 67.

Hay, Alexander, of Arnbath
Son of Alexander Hay of Arnbath, who was son of George Hay of Rannes and his wife, Agnes Guthrie, daughter of the Bishop of Moray.

Hay, Alexander, younger of Arnbath
Was imprisoned and claimed to have been forced to join the Jacobite cause. After his release he went abroad and in his sixties was said to be a very rich man, probably by selling Spa water.

Hay, Alexander, conjunct Sheriff-Clerk, Aberdeen
One of the sons of Thomas Hay, Sheriff-Clerk and his wife, Jean King. Had brother called Colin.

Hay, Charles, of Rannes
Eldest son of James Hay of Rannes and his wife, Margaret Gordon of Glengerack. Born in 1688. In 1710 he married Helen, only child of Dr Andrew Fraser of Inverness, and by her had two sons, of whom the elder, Andrew, took part in the '45, and five daughters. Died in London in 1751.

Hay, John, of Muldavit
Son of William Hay of Muldavit and his wife, Helen Crichton, sister of James, Viscount Frendraught, whom he married in 1663. Married

Katherine, eldest daughter of James Hay of Rannes in 1697. Died in 1720.

Hay, John, Barber

Met at Mistress Hepburn's house on 22 September (see William Hepburn).

Hay, Walter, of Lickleyhead

Brother of the Laird of Arnbath, and uncle of young Alexander Hay. He was dead by 18 Dec 1725, when his son, Alexander, was served heir to him.

Hay, William, Messenger

Met at Mistress Hepburn's house on 22 September (see William Hepburn).

Hay, The Rev William, Minister of Rothiemay

Married twice, but the name of his first wife is unknown though he had two sons and two daughters by her. His second wife, whom he married on 7 May 1700 was Ann, daughter of William Grant of Crichie. He was described at one point as "a scandalous drunkard." He died in January 1718.

Henderson, Robert

Tenant of David Lumsden of Cushnie "forced to be in the Rebellion by the threats and force of the Earl of Mar" and taken prisoner at Preston in November 1715 with 12 other tenants of David Lumsden or Harry Lumsden of Auchindoir and Robert Reid of Mid Clove. Transported from Liverpool to Virginia on *Friendship* 24 May 1716, landed in Maryland Aug 1716.

Hepburn, The Rev Alexander, Episcopal Minister of St Fergus and Peterhead

A native of Buchan. He married Eliza Clark, who died in 1703, and had two sons and three daughters. He died in Peterhead in 1737, aged about 81, and left behind him in manuscript a decription of Buchan in 1721.

Hepburn, William, Vintner, Merchant

On 22 September, a mob first met in Mistress Hepburn's and then came to the counsel house and required the armes and amunitions belonging to the town with the Keys of the Block house, seeing they were not to regard the magistrates any longer as magistrates."

Horn, John, of Westhall

Son of Rev James Horn and his wife Isobella, daughter of John Leslie, 7th of Pitcapel. Maried first Anna, daughter of Robert, 2nd Viscount Arbuthnott on 20 Nov 1693, and had a daughter, Anna. His second wife was Anna Simpson.

Hunter, The Rev William, Minister of Banff

Born about 1662, the son of Robert Hunter, Provost of Ayr and Martha Musket of Craighead, Perthshire. He married twice: (1) 27 Dec 1699, Anne, daughter of John Guthrie of King Edward and widow of Patrick Grant of Dunlugas, by whom he had a son Alexander, and other Children: (2) in 1723, Mary Ogilvie, daughter of George, 3rd Lord Banff, and widow of John Joass of Colleonard. He died in 1730.

Idell, The Rev William, Minister of Coull

Born in Mar, he was schoolmaster of Chapel of Garioch in 1669.

Innes, Sir George, of Coxton

Son of Sir Alexander Innes, 1st Baronet of Coston and his first wife, Jean Rollo of Bannockburn. Married in 1706 Elizabeth, daughter of John Gordon of Rothiemay and his wife, Elizabeth Barclay, heiress of Towie. He had three sons, Alexander, John and James. Died at Scone in 1715, it is believed of wounds received at Sheriffmuir.

Innes, Colonel James 1715 & 1745

Third son of Sir Alexander Innes, 1st Baronet of Coston. Also involved in the '45 when almost 70 years old, and was executed on 21 Oct 1746 at Brampton. He left a wife, Mary Ramsay, and several daughters.

Innes, John, of Sinnahard

Son of John Innes of Towie, Culquoich and Sinnahard, he was the 4th Innes owner of Sinnahard and married in 1712 Anne Hay of Arnbath. Died 1725.

Innes, The Rev John, Minister of Gamrie

Was at King's College, Aberdeen in 1667. He married Margaret Gordon, who, with a daughter, survived him. He died on 14 June 1732, aged 82.

Innes, Father Lewis, Catholic Priest

Born in Walkerdale in the Enzie in 1651, was the second son of James Innes, 1st of Drumgask and his wife, Jane, daughter of Robert Robertson, Provost of Aberdeen. Sent to the Scots College in Paris, and in 1682 became its Principal. Confidential Secretary to Mary of Modena, Consort of King James VII. He died in Paris on 22 January 1738.

Irvine, Adam, of Brucklay 1715 & 1745

Son of the Rev Robert Irvine, Minister of Towie, and his second wife, Agnes, daughter of Patrick Murray of Blairfindy. Married in 1710, Margaret, daughter of Sir John Reid, 1st Baronet of Barra. He left two sons and two daughters.

Irvine, Alexander, younger of Drum

Son of Alexander Irvine of Murtle and his wife, Janet, daughter of Alexander Irvine of Drum. Died unmarried in 1735.

Irvine, James, Sheriff-Clerk of Kincardine

Son of Robert Irvine and Barbara Mitchell, his wife. Grandson of John Irvine "in Seattoun". He was married, with at least one son.

Irvine, John, of Kingcausie

Son of John Irvine of Kingcausie, who died in 1714 and his wife, Elizabeth, daughter of John Ramsay of Clush. Married Margaret, daughter of Thomas Forbes, merchant in Aberdeen by whom he had five sons and four daughters born between the years 1703 and 1723. His wife died on 30 December 1764 aged 83.

Irvine, John, Catholic Priest

Born in 1652, and in 1671 went to the Scots College in Rome. He left in 1679 and was for many years a missionary in Scotland, dying at Gordon Castle, 17 April 1717.

Irvine, William, of Artamford
Second son of James Irvine of Artamford and his wife, Margaret, daughter of James Sutherland of Kinminity, Keith.

Irvine, The Rev William, of Fortrie
Son of Alexander Irvine of Fortrie, parish of Ellon, he was born there about 1660. A strong Jacobite, he was present at Killiecrankie. He escaped from both Dundee and Fleet prisons, and lived subsequently in Linlithgow. He is described as being "of a forward and fiery temper, rough and blustering." He died in Edinburgh on 19 December 1725.

Jaffray, Andrew, of Ardtannies
Son of Provost Alexander Jaffray and his wife, Sarah Cant. A merchant in Aberdeen, he had a wife and ten children.

Jaffray, The Rev Andrew, Minister of Alford
Probably son of Alexander Jaffray, Minister of King Edward. Ordained deacon in 1674, he was deposed on 26 September 1716 for espousing the Jacobite cause. He married Marjory Davidson and had four sons.

Johnston, Sir John, of Caskieben
Son of John Johnston of New Place. His wife was Janet, daughter of Thomas Mitchell of Tilliegreig, Baillie of Aberdeen, and he had two daughters and an only son John, who predeceased him.

Johnston, John, younger of Caskieben
Only son of John Johnston born in 1690. Killed at Sheriffmuir.

Johnston, John, of Boginjoss
Second son of John Johnston of Bishopstown, Newhills, and his wife, Margaret Alexander. Married Christian Marnoch, by whom he had three sons and one daughter. He died in 1721.

Jollie, William
Jacobite at Fraserburgh where the town was searched for the arms left by Lord Lovat and John Forbes of Culloden. These were delivered to George Keith, younger of Ludquharn.

Keith, Alexander, of Northfield
Eldest son of George Keith of Northfield. Married Sophia, eldest daughter of John Fraser of Memsie, before 1693. Had at least two sons, Alexander and John, and one daughter, Anne.

Keith, George, Advocate, Aberdeen
Second son of Sir William Keith of Ludquharn. Died 24 Sept 1738.

Keith, The Rev James, Belhelvie

Keith, James
Born 16 Jun 1696 son of William Keith, Earl Marischal. Died Hochkirchen 14 Oct 1758.

Keith, John
Tenant of the Earl of Aboyne.

Keith, The Rev John, of Glasgowego

Keith, Sir William, of Ludquharn
Son and heir of Sir Alexander, 2nd Baronet of Ludquharn. Married a daughter of George Smith of Rapness and by her had two sons and

one daughter, Mary.   William, the elder son was from 1716 to 1726 Governor of Pennsylvania.

Kintore, William, 2nd Earl of
Eldest son of Sir John Keith.   His wife Catharine was daughter of the 4th Viscount Stormont.   His eldest son John, at 26 fought with his father at Sheriffmuir and was married to the daughter of Lord Grange (brother of the Earl of Mar whose wife was so mysteriously imprisoned on St Kilda). His younger son, William died without issue.

Law, The Rev Alexander, Minister of Kearn
Ordained Minister of Kearn on 31 March 1713 and deposed 4 April 1716.

Law, The Rev William, Minister of Slains
Appointed schoolmaster at Strichen in 1679.   He was suspended from the ministry for erroneous doctrine.

Leith, Alexander, of Freefield
Second son of James Leith of New Leslie, afterwards of Leith Hall. He married Christian, daughter of Alexander Davidson of Newton, by whom he had four sons, Alexander, Walter, Patrick and George.   He died on 4 April 1754, aged 90.

Leith, George, Secretary to Lord Erroll
Jacobite at Fraserburgh where the town was searched for the arms left by Lord Lovat and John Forbes of Culloden. These were delivered to George Keith, younger of Ludquharn.

Leith, John, of Leith Hall
Eldest son of James Leith of New Leslie, Peil Syde, Arnbog, etc and Margaret Strachan of Glenkindie. Married Janet, daughter of George, 2nd Lord Banff and had five sons. Died in 1727.

Leith, The Rev Patrick, Minister of Lumphanan
Graduated at King's College, Aberdeen, 11 July 1676 and deposed on 4 September 1716 for engaging in the Rising.

Leslie, Charles "Mussel-Mou'd Charlie" 1715 & 1745
So called from a singular projection of his under-lip.   He was born in 1667, a natural son of Leslie of Pitcaple.   A ballad monger, described as a thin man, about 5 feet 10 inches in height, with small fiery eyes, a long chin and red hair.   Died at Old Rayne in 1782 at the extraordinary age of 105 - probably the last survivor of the Rising of 1715.

Leslie, The Rev Charles, of Glasslough
The family of Leslie of Glasslough, Ireland is descended from the Wardes' branch of the family of Leslie of Balquhain.   Born 17 July 1650 sixth son of Rev Charles Leslie, admitted to Trinity College, Dublin in 1664.   He married Jane Leslie and had two sons, Robert and Henry.

Leslie, James, of the Warthill family
Eldest son of Alexander Leslie, Minister of Crail in Fife, and his wife Helen, daughter of John Seymour, Minister of Macgill.   Married Catherine Mills, and died in 1730, having had three sons and three daughters.

Leslie, John, Baillie, Aberdeen
   Probably died around 18 September 1730.
Leslie, The Rev William, of Little Folla
   Eldest son of George Leslie, 4th Laird of Little Folla and his wife,
   Isabella, daughter of William Cheyne of Kaithen.   Sometime
   schoolmaster at Auchterless, he went to Ireland to assist his uncle in
   Fermanagh.   He retired to Little Folla and died in 1722, aged 71.
Liddell, George, Professor of Mathematics, Marischal College, Aberdeen
   Son of Duncan Liddell and his wife Jean Montgomery.
Lindsay, William, Goldsmith, Aberdeen
   Taxer appointed by the Town of Aberdeen.   Deacon-Convenor of the
   Incorporated Trades in 1713.
Lister, John, of Clerkseat
   The son of Alexander Lister, Regent of Marischal College in 1682,
   John Lister was there from 1697 to 1701.   Married Jean Gordon and
   had at least one son, Thomas.
Livingstone, The Rev Andrew, Minister of Keig
   Married, he had three sons and one daughter, William, Andrew,
   Alexander and Margaret.
Livingstone, The Rev William, Minister of Deer
   Ejected from the church in 1711, he took part in the 'Rabbling of Deer'.
   During the Rising of 1715 he "invaded" the church of Deer and prayed
   for the Old Chevalier and the success of his arms.   He died in 1751.
Logan, John
   Jacobite at Fraserburgh where the town was searched for the arms left
   by Lord Lovat and John Forbes of Culloden.   These were delivered to
   George Keith, younger of Ludquharn.
Longmoor, William, Schoolmaster of Rothiemay
Lumsden, David, of Cushnie
   Third son of Alexander Lumsden, 13th Laird of Cushnie and his
   second wife Elizabeth Leith of Whitehaugh.   Born in 1682, he married
   Margaret, sister of Sir William Forbes of Craigievar, by whom he had
   one daughter, Margaret.   He died on 23 December 1718.
Lumsden, Harry, younger of Auchindoir
   Born in 1685, the eldest son of John Lumsden of Auchindoir and
   Corrachree, who married Agnes, daughter of Gordon of Auchlyne and
   Knockespock.   Transported from Liverpool to Virginia on the
   Friendship 24 May 1716, landed Maryland Aug 1716, he returned to
   Scotland after two years.   He married, firstly in 1720 Katherine,
   daughter of George Gordon of Buckie (she died in 1733) by whom he
   had at least two sons, John, Matthew and three daughters, and
   secondly, in 1736 Margaret, sister of Sir Archibald Foulis of Dunipace
   and widow of Peter Gordon of Ardmeallie, by whom there was no
   issue.   Died in 8 June 1754, aged 69.
Lunan, The Rev Alexander, Minister of Daviot
   Succeeded his father, the Rev William Lunan as Minister, and married
   Janet, daughter of Sir James Elphinstone of Logie.   He died in 1731.
McGie, James
   In Waterton, Aberdeenshire.

McGregor, Alexander

Younger brother of Callum McGregor in Richaharne.   Tenant of the Earl of Aboyne.

McGregor (or Gregory), Callum or Malcolm, in Richaharne (now Reinacham)

Tenant of the Earl of Aboyne.   In 1696 he had three sons, Grigor, John and Archibald.

McGregor, John

Younger brother of Callum McGregor in Richaharne.   Tenant of the Earl of Aboyne.

McHardy, John, in Glengairn

Tenant of the Earl of Aboyne.   In 1696 he was married to Margaret Ochterlonie and had a son, David.

McHenry, George, Collector of Cess, Aberdeen

Mackenzie, James

Son of Kenneth of Dalmore, served heir to his father on 29 June 1723. In 1728 married Isobel, daughter of John Douglas of Tilquhilly, and died before 1733 leaving one child, Agnes.

Mackenzie, Kenneth, of Dalmore

Owner of Mar Lodge.   Married with two children.

Maitland, The Rev David, Episcopal Minister of Forgue

Third son of the Rev John Maitland, Minister of Inverkeithny.   It is stated he lost his sight about 1734, but continued to discharge the duties of the ministry though blind, and again recovered his sight on undergoing an operation for cataract.

Maitland, The Rev James, Minister of Inverkeithny

Born in 1671, he was the eldest son of the Rev John Maitland, also Minister of Inverkeithny, whom he succeeded.| He was present as Chaplain at Culloden in 1745.

Maitland, The Rev John, Minister of Forgue

Younger brother of the Rev James Maitland, Minister of Inverkeithny, he was ordained Minister of Insch on 26 April 1703.   He married Christian Ramsay, and died 16 April 1740, in his 69th year.

Maitland, The Rev Richard, Minister of Nigg

Schoolmaster at Foveran in 1671, he married three times (1) Susanna, daughter of Rev Alexander Irvine, Minister of Longside; (2) Katherine, daughter of the Rev John Milne, Minister of Fetteresso, and had issue 15 children; and (3) Mary, daughter of the Rev George Keith, Minister of Old Deer.   He died in 1719.

Marr, George, Merchant

On the Burgess Roll of Aberdeen in 1700.   He survived the Rising.

Martin, Peter

Servant to John Hamilton of Gibston, discharged from Newgate in Dec 1716.

Maule, George, Factor for the Earl of Panmure

Son of Patrick Maule and Christian Forbes.   Married to Susan Stuart they had James, baptized on 30 Aug 1696, Henry, baptized in 1698 and John, baptized in 1700.

Menzies, Charles, of Kinmundy
The owner of this estate in 1715.

Menzies, William, of Pitfodels
Son of Gilbert Menzies, 4th Laird of Pitfodels and Beatrix Fletcher. Born in 1688, educated at the Scots College at Douai from 1700-1707, married Mary, eldest daughter of John Urquhart of Meldrum, and had six sons, all Jacobites of '45. Died on 6 January 1780 being 92, and his wife, Mary, died 20 April 1771, aged 80.

Meston, William
Born in Midmar about 1680, son of William Meston, blacksmith and Katherine Leonard. MA degree from Marischal College, he became a Regent and appointed Professor of Philosophy in 1713, but was deposed after the Rising. He died in 1745.

Middleton, Captain Alexander
One of the fourteen sons of the Rev George Middleton, born in 1676. Married to Elspet Burnett in 1705. He died on 26 October 1751.

Middleton, The Rev George, Principal of King's College, Aberdeen
Eldest son of Dr Alexander Middleton, Principal of King's College, Aberdeen. Was baptized 25 February 1645. He married Janet Gordon, and had by her fourteen sons and four daughters! He died May 1726 in his 82nd year and his sturdy widow survived him until 1753, when she passed away at the age of 101.

Mitchell, Thomas, of Thainston
Born in 1659, he was the second son of Baillie Thomas Mitchell of Tilliegreig by his second wife, Marjory Moir. He married three times, first in 1692 to Janet, daughter of Sir Patrick Leslie of Eden, secondly Isabella, sister of Alexander Paton, afterwards Provost of Aberdeen, and thirdly Jean Mercer. He died in December 1719, leaving at least one son Thomas, who died in 1721. His only daughter was named Barbara.

Moir, Alexander, of Scotstown
Son of Dr William Moir of Scotstown and Spital who married Jean daughter of Alexander Abernethy, 1st of Mayen. He married Mary Chalmers and had two sons, William and George, and two daughters, Janet and Jean. He died in 1752.

Moir, Alexander, Regent, Marischal College, Aberdeen
Second son of John Moir, 1st of Stoneywood. In the Poll Book of 1696 it states that he had no wife, child or servants.

Moir, James, 2nd of Stoneywood
Brother of Alexander Moir, Regent. Eldest son of John Moir, 1st of Stoneywood and his wife Jean, eldest daughter of James Sandilands, 1st of Cotton. Baptized in Aberdeen, 1 Sept 1659. MP for Aberdeenshire from 1689-1707. He married twice, on 10 July 1683, Mary, eldest daughter of the Rev William Scroggie, Bishop of Argyll, issue four sons, the eldest being James, and three daughters. Secondly, Jean, daughter of Alexander Abernethy, 1st of Mayen and widow of William Moir of Scotstown. By her he had three sons, one of whom was William Moir of Lonmay, and two daughters. Jean

Abernethy died in Nov 1749 aged 85. He died on 22 Nov 1739 aged 80.

Moir, James, younger, and 3rd of Stoneywood
Son of James, 2nd of Stoneywood and his first wife, Mary Scroggie. He married Jean, daughter of William Erskine, 6th of Pittodrie, and had five sons and two daughters. It is asserted that he survived until 1782.

Moir, William, of Invernetty, Peterhead
Third son of John Moir, 1st of Stoneywood, born in 1669. Became merchant in Aberdeen. He married Christian Guthrie in 1710 and then Jean, daughter of Colonel Lewis Hay by whom he had two sons, James and William. His Will is in the Commissariot of Aberdeen for 22 Dec 1744.

Moir, William
Tenant of David Lumsden of Cushnie "forced to be in the Rebellion by the threats and force of the Earl of Mar" and taken prisoner at Preston in November 1715 with 12 other tenants of David Lumsden or Harry Lumsden of Auchindoir and Robert Reid of Mid Clove. Transported to Virginia in 1716.

Moir, William, Bursar, King's College, Aberdeen
"On Thursday, 1 February 1716 came up the street of the old towne with the picture of the Duke of Brunswick fixed behind the musle and the Ramer of his gun. He was one of those who had a gun, and who afterwards committed disorders at Alexander Taylor's house in Cotton and took away his armes."

Mowat, William, Merchant, Aberdeen
Taxer appointed by the Town of Aberdeen.

Murray, The Rev William, Minister of Inverurie
A native of the Garioch, he was at King's College, Aberdeen in 1667. He married Magdalen Gellie and had five children.

Niven, Thomas, Merchant
One of the merchants of Aberdeen from whom the Government took gunpowder to send to Edinburgh.

Ogilvie, Archibald of Rothiemay
Son of Sir Patrick Ogilvie, Lord Boyne, by his second wife, Anne Douglas of Whittinghame. Born about 1680, he married Isobel, third daughter of the Rev George Meldrum, Minister of Glass and his wife Jean Duff of Keithmore. He had sons James and Patrick and a daughter Mary. He died abroad in or before 1736.

Ogilvie, James, of Boyne
Eldest son of Sir Patrick Ogilvie of Boyne, and his first wife Anna Grant, he was born in 1667. He married in 1688, Anna, daughter of Major George Arnot of Grange in Fife, by whom he had a son James and one daughter. He married secondly, a Frenchwoman of the name Busilie, by whom he had a son, John Lewis.

Ogilvie, James, younger of Boyne
Son of James Ogilvie of Boyne and his first wife Anna Arnot. Lived mostly with his father in France, returning for the Rising. He never married, and died at Rouen in 1717.

Ogilvie, John, Bursar, King's College, Aberdeen
Expelled for seditious practices 30 April 1716. He and his brother
Patrick, a year older, with William Moir, came to the house of William
Walker, the Town's Drummer, and forced him to go out with his drum
and make proclamation, "desiring all persons to come and see the
Duke of Brunswick burnt in effigie."

Ogilvie, Patrick, Aberdeen

Ogilvie, William, Chamberlain to the Earl of Erroll
Nothing is known of his family. He was certified to be dangerously ill
after Sheriffmuir, and subsequently died in Edinburgh Castle of
asthma and heart failure.

Ogilvie, William, the Earl of Erroll's chamberlain
Jacobite at Fraserburgh where the town was searched for the arms left
by Lord Lovat and John Forbes of Culloden. These were delivered to
George Keith, younger of Ludquham.

Oliphant, Colonel The Hon William
Third son of Patrick, 6th Lord Oliphant and his wife Mary, daughter of
James Crichton of Frendraught. He married Marie Magdeleine Elinga
of Frisian extraction. He had a son or sons who predeceased him,
and a daughter, Marie Jean Baptiste, who was married at Orleans on
19 Nov 1710 to Louis Grenolias, sieur de Cornou.

Ord, John, of Findochty
Eldest son of William Otd of Findochty and his wife, Jean Innes. He
married Elizabeth, daughter of Sir Alexander Innes of Coxton
(Contract of Marriage 9 Aug 1710).

Park, Captain James, Shipmaster, Peterhead
It was in his house that the Chevalier slept the first night on his arrival
in Peterhead, 22 Dec 1715. It is said that he carried the Royal
Personage ashore on his back. He married in 1714, Janet, youngest
daughter of Alexander Arbuthnot, Dyer in Peterhead, and widow of
John Dalgarno of Mill of Rora. They had a daughter Ann. Their son
was Rev Charles Cordiner, Minister of the Episcopal Church in Banff.
He died on 26 May 1739 aged 59.

Paterson, Robert, Principal of Marischal College
Younger son of John, Bishop of Ross. He was married by 1696 and
had eight children.

Paton, Alexander, of Kinaldie
Son of Alexander Paton, Provost, and his first wife Elizabeth Urquhart.
He was a pupil in Sept 1700.

Paton, John, of Grandhome
Eldest son of George Paton, Advocate, and his wife Isabella Christie.
Born in 1675, he married twice, first at Troup House on 31 Jan 1710 to
Margaret, (died 6 Mar 1715) eldest daughter of Alexander Garden of
Troup, and had a son, George. Secondly he married Christian,
daughter of John Forbes of Leslie. He died 5 Aug 1739.

Peacock, George, Regent of Marischal College, Aberdeen
He married Elizabeth, daughter of Dr James Leslie, and is mentioned
in the Poll Book (1696) with his wife and three children.

Pirie, George, Periwigmaker in Fraserburgh

A warrant had been issued for his arrest, but he was allowed bail on promising he would "carrie himself Loyally to his Majesty King George."

Pittendrigh, Robert, Merchant, Aberdeen

He had married before Aug 1715, Sophia, daughter of John Forbes of Auchanth. He survived the Rising.

Rae, James

Tenant of David Lumsden of Cushnie "forced to be in the Rebellion by the threats and force of the Earl of Mar" and taken prisoner at Preston in November 1715 with 12 other tenants of David Lumsden or Harry Lumsden of Auchindoir and Robert Reid of Mid Clove. Transported from Liverpool to Jamaica or Virginia on *Elizabeth and Anne* 29 Jun 1716, landed at York, Virginia.

Ramsay, The Rev Gilbert, Minister of Dyce

Son of Robert Ramsay, merchant of Aberdeen, at Marischal College in 1673. His wife was Jean Livingstone, by whom he had a daughter, Anna. He died 31 May 1728.

Ramsay, William

Jacobite at Fraserburgh where the town was searched for the arms left by Lord Lovat and John Forbes of Culloden. These were delivered to George Keith, younger of Ludquharn.

Reid, Alexander, Alford, Aberdeenshire

Transported from Liverpool to Maryland on *Friendship* 24 May 1716, settled Reidbourne, Chester River, Calvert County, Maryland. Died 14 Oct 1718.

Reid, The Rev John, Minister of Durris

Schoolmaster of Banchory-Ternan, he was made clerk to the Session in 1670. He married twice (1) Isabel Fraser, (2) Margaret Cruden, who survived him. He died before 2 Apr 1728.

Reid, Peter, Catholic Priest

Son of Alexander Reid and Isabella Brebner, and educated at the Scots College in Rome. He returned to Scotland in 1709 and died at Presholme in 1726.

Reid, Robert, of Mid Clova

The grandfather of Robert was the younger brother of James Reid of Bourtie, and son of Alexander of New Milne. Transported from Liverpool to to Virginia on *Elizabeth and Anne*, and still there in 1723.

Ried, William, Merchant in Aberdeen

Reid, William, Messenger

Met at Mistress Hepburn's house on 22 September (see William Hepburn).

Rickart, David, of Rickarton

Second son of George Rickart of Arnage and Auchnacant by his wife, Janet, daughter of Sir William Forbes of Monymusk. He married Katharine Arbuthnott, daughter of Robert, 2nd Viscount Arbuthnott and widow of Robert Gordon of Cluny, by whom he had one son John, and two daughters. He died 29 July 1718, aged 51.

Ritchie, Andrew, of Foresterhill
Taxer appointed by the Town of Aberdeen.

Ritchie, John, younger, Shipmaster in Fraserburgh
A warrant had been issued for his arrest, but he was allowed bail on promising he would "carrie himself Loyally to his Majesty King George."

Ritchie, Malcolm
Tenant of the Earl of Aboyne.

Robertson, The Rev Alexander, Fochabers
In September 1716 "Att Elgin.   The Presbytery complained of the various encroachments made upon their ministry by Episcopal preachers, eg Alexander Robertson, who kept a meeting-house."

Robertson, The Rev Alexander, Minister of Longside
Son of Rev Thomas Robertson, Minister of Longside, was presented to Longside (as assistant and successor to his father) in 1687.   He was proprietor of Downiehills, Peterhead and is mentioned as having seen a mermaid!   He married Christian, daughter of John Mercer, Minister of Kinnellar, and had three sons and one daughter.

Robertson, George
Taxer for the Town of Aberdeen.   Was Deacon of the Shoemakers and Convener of the Incorporated Trades in 1726 and 1727.

Robertson, James
Jacobite at Fraserburgh where the town was searched for the arms left by Lord Lovat and John Forbes of Culloden.   These were delivered to George Keith, younger of Ludquharn.

Robertson, The Rev John, Episcopal Minister, Strathdon
Sometime schoolmaster of Strathdon, and on 24 July 1681 was ordained Minister of that parish.

Robertson, William
Younger brother of Alexander, the Laird, and son of Rev Thomas Robertson, Minister of Longside.

Roper, Thomas, Schoolmaster of Rhynie
On his tombstone is says "Here lyes Mr Thomas Roper, who was sometime Schoolmaster at Rhynie, lawful husband to Jean Innes, who died 9 March 174-, aged 81".

Rose, The Rev Alexander, of Cairnie
Fourth son of David Rose of Earlsmill, near Darnaway (a branch of the Kilravock family).   Minister of Cairnie from 1680 to 1716 when he was deposed for reading the Chevalier's Proclamation from his pulpit. Described as "courageous, firm of purpose, of good judgement, and although choleric not vindictive."   He married Ann, daughter of James Gordon of Daach, and had five sons and two daughters.   He lived to a great age.

Rose, Alexander, of Lethenty
Eldest son of the Rev John Rose of Insch, Minister of Foveran and his wife Isobel, dauthter of John Udny of Udny.   He married Anne, daughter of Alexander Forbes of Ballogie, by whom he had three sons and four daughters.

Rose, David, Schoolmaster, Cairnie
While occupying this position he joined the Jacobite army in 1715 and went south.

Rose, John, of Allanbuie
Married Elizabeth, daughter of Alexander Gordon, 4th of Arradoul.

Rose, (or Ross), The Rev Patrick, Episcopalian Minister of Arbroath
Uncle of William Rose, Factor to James, 2nd Earl of Fife.

Ross, John, Mill of Denety
Son of Alexander Ross who was at Mill of Denety (Dinnet) in 1667.

Ross, John
Son of a Bishop or Archbishop.

Ross, Peter, tailor in Braemar
Captured by the Dutch near Burntisland 11 January 1716

Sandilands, Patrick, Sheriff-Depute of Aberdeenshire
Eldest son of Patrick Sandilands of Cotton and Margaret Ord. His wife was Barbara, daughter of William Cumine of Pitullie, but she died without issue.

Scott, Alexander, Shipmaster, Aberdeen
The Poll Book (1696) gives "Alexander Scot, Skiper for himselfe, no wife, child, nor servant; his brother, William Scot, ane boy."

Sempill, Robert, Titular Lord Sempill
Father of the Jacobite Lord Sempill

Shand, Thomas, Merchant, Aberdeen
Was probably a younger son of Thomas Shand of Craig, near Dyce, Treasurer of Aberdeen 1672-78, and his wife Anna Duncan. Married Isobel, only daughter of Thomas Hay, Sheriff-Clerk of Aberdeen. His Will is dated 1748.

Shand, William, servant to the Laird of Mayen
One of the prisoners in Stirling, taken at Sheriffmuir, which goes to show that his master was probably also present at the battle, with Huntly's Foot.

Shaw, Patrick, servant to John Abernethy of Mayen.
A prisoner at Stirling.

Shirrefs, Alexander, Drumnagour, Kildrummy
Son of James Shirrefs, farmer, of Little Miln (on the estate of Lord Forbes) and his wife, Christian Blair, living at Cornabo (probably a farm of that name in the parish of Monymusk). He married three times, but only the name of his second wife, Agnes Ferrier, is known. By his first wife he had four sons, and by his second a daughter and two sons.

Sibbald, The Rev James, Keith
In the Kirk Session Records of Keith, 1716, he is called "the Scandalous Trumpeter of Rebellion and late Preacher of the Episcopal Meeting House in the Parish."

Simpson, William, Baillie, Aberdeen
Married at Aberdeen, 11 Sept 1699, Mary, daughter of David Aedie, of Newark and Easter-Echt, Aberdeenshire and had at least one daughter, Sarah.

Sinclair, George, Merchant, Aberdeen
   Taxer appointed by the Town of Aberdeen.
Sivewright, James, Westertown, Huntly
Skene, James, Captain, of Halyards, Fife
   From the Aberdeenshire family.   Fifth son of John Skene, 4th of
   Halyards, and his wife Elizabeth, second daughter of Sir Thomas
   Wallace, Baronet of Craigie.   He married Mary Ann, daughter of the
   Rev J. Smith of Battersea, and died in 1736 leaving two sons and one
   daughter.
Smith, Alexander, Merchant
   Jacobite at Fraserburgh where the town was searched for the arms left
   by Lord Lovat and John Forbes of Culloden.   These were delivered to
   George Keith, younger of Ludquharn.
Smith, The Rev Alexander, Episcopal Minister, Bellie
Smith, Joram, Barber
   Met at Mistress Hepburn's house on 22 September (see William
   Hepburn).
Smith, Patrick, Junior, of Inveramsay
   Son of John Smith of Inveramsay, who died in 1750 aged nearly 100.
   He married on 8 November 1705, Elizabeth, daughter of Alexander
   Kerr of Menie, and had three sons and six daughters.   He died in
   1743.
Smith, Robert
   Jacobite at Fraserburgh where the town was searched for the arms left
   by Lord Lovat and John Forbes of Culloden.   These were delivered to
   George Keith, younger of Ludquharn.
Smith, William, Regent of Marischal College, Aberdeen
   The Poll Book (1696) states that he had then "no wife, child, nor
   servant."
Smith, William, Merchant
   Taxer appointed by the Town of Aberdeen.
Souper, William, of Gilcomiston, Merchant, Aberdeen
   Son of John Souper, merchant burgess of Aberdeen, and his wife,
   Margaret Clark.   Married in 1685, Jean, eldest daughter of James
   Byres of Coates, by whom he had eight sons and four daughters.
   Died in Aberdeen, 20 Sep 1724, aged 63.
Southest, James, 5th Earl of
   Only son of Charles, 4th Earl of Southesk, and Lady Mary Maitland,
   second daughter of Charles, 3rd Earl of Lauderdale.   He was born 4
   April 1692 and succeeded when only a child of 8.   He had a wife and
   children.
Speediman, David, Glover, Aberdeen
   Convener of Trades.   He was married to Christian Adamson and had
   at least two sons, William and James.
Spence, William, Hook-maker
   In 1713, he had been Master of the Trades Hospitality Charity, also he
   met at Mistress Hepburn's house on 22 September (see William
   Hepburn).

Stewart, Andrew, of Auchlunkart
Eldest son of Patrick Stewart of Tanachie and his wife, Anna, daughter of Thomas Gordon of Myretown. Married 5 Dec 1706, Helen, daughter and heiress of Walter Innes of Auchlunkart. He died 17 Sept 1719 leaving a son, Alexander.

Stewart, Gordon
Second son of Patrick Stewart of Tanachie. Married in 1722, Anne, daughter of Sir James Abercromby, Baronet of Birkenbog, and died in Dec 1748, leaving two sons and two daughters.

Stewart, James
This was the man who supplied meal to Rannes.

Stewart, John, of Drumin
Married in 1702 to Elizabeth, daughter of George Forbes, 3rd of Skellater, and had at least two sons, Charles and Gordon. There was also one daughter, Isabella.

Stewart, John, in Ballaterach
Factor to the Earl of Aboyne, and brother of William Stewart of Aucholzie.

Stewart, John, of Boggs
Younger brother of Andrew Stewart, 4th of Tanachie. Married before 4 Nov 1697, Jean Gordon of Farskane.

Stewart, Captain John, of Dens and Crichie
Son of Colonel James Stewart, described as "of the Mearns," but of whom not much is known except hat the came of the family of Stewart of Kilcoy, Ross-shire. He married Agnes, born 1661, (died 1729), daughter of Gilbert Gray, who lived at Shivas. It is alleged that she was so plain that the Earl of Moray said he would rather pay £500 than marry her! The issue was a son, John, born in 1703, who died unmarried in 1749, and a daughter, Theodosia, born at Inverness in 1701 and died 1769. He died in 1729.

Stewart, Robert, Late Provost
Son of Alexander Stewart of Newhall, Fife, born 1670. Married Anne, daughter of John Gordon, Provost, and had two sons and four daughters. Died on 10 Mar 1749, aged 78.

Stewart, William, of Aucholzie
Married twice, first to Barbara Farquhar by whom he had a daughter; secondly to Eupham, daughter of Harry Farquharson of Whitehouse, by whom he had three sons and four daughters. He died about 1727.

Strachan, Alexander, Merchant, Aberdeen
There were several of this name in Aberdeen at the time.

Strachan, The Rev Sir James, Baronet of Thornton
Eldest son of Sir James Strachan, 3rd Baronet and his second wife, Elizabeth, third daughter of Thomas Forbes of Waterton. He married twice (1) Katherine Rose, who died in 1680; (2) in 1681, Barbara Forbes of Waterton (niece of his father's second wife). James, his eldest son, predeceased his father and is believed to have been killed during the Rising of 1715, and another brother, Francis, is stated to have followed the fortunes of the Stuarts, lived in Paris and taken Orders. Died at Inverness in 1715 aged about 75.

Strachan, Thomas, Baillie, Aberdeen
His Will is in the Commissariot 13 December 1738, with that of his daughter, Margaret.

Strachan, William

Swan, The Rev William, Minister of Pitsligo
Son of Rev Alexander Swan, Minister of Pitsligo and his first wife, Jean Leslie. Took a degree at King's College, Aberdeen in 1679. He married Grizel Robertson and had two sons, Alexander and William. In 1742 he was aged eighty-four, and died soon afterwards.

Taus, Charles
Tenant of the Earl of Aboyne.

Taylor, John
Jacobite at Fraserburgh where the town was searched for the arms left by Lord Lovat and John Forbes of Culloden. These were delivered to George Keith, younger of Ludquharn.

Thompson, Andrew
Taxer appointed by the Town of Aberdeen.

Thompson, Patrick, Under Master, Grammar School, Aberdeen

Thomson, John
Jacobite at Fraserburgh where the town was searched for the arms left by Lord Lovat and John Forbes of Culloden. These were delivered to George Keith, younger of Ludquharn

Thomson, William
Collector of Cess at Cullen.

Tulloch, David
The very much younger half-brother of Thomas Tulloch of Tannachy, David was the fifth son of Alexander Tulloch by his second wife, Margaret Simpson.

Turner, John of Turnerhall
Eldest son of Robert Turner, 1st of Turnerhall and Margaret Rose, born in 1694. He married Margaret, daughter of Farquharson of Westone, Tarland, and had three sons and three daughters. Died in 1756.

Turner, Robert, 1st of Turnerhall
Fourth son of Andrew Turner of Kinminity in Birse. Married Margaret in 1693, eldest daughter of John Rose of Rosehill. They had nine sons and seven daughters. Died in 1741.

Tyrie, David, of Dunnydeer
Eldest son of John Tyrie of Dunnydeer and his wife, Margaret Tulloch of Tanachie, Morayshire. He married firstly Elizabeth Gordon of Rothiemay by whom he had three daughters, and secondly, Anna Menzies of Pitfodels, by whom there were three sons and two daughters. He died in 1750.

Urquhart, Colonel James
Son of Johnathan Urquhart of Cromarty and Lady Jean Graham, grand-daughter of the great Montrose. He married Anne Rollo of Powhouse, and had one daughter, Grizel. He died of face cancer in 1741.

Urquhart, Dr James, Regent of King's College, Aberdeen
Son of Dr Patrick Urquhart, Professor of Medicine.

Urquhart, John, afterwards of Craigston
The only son of James Urquhart of Knockleith and his wife, Margaret Fraser of Easter Tyrie, he was born at Knockleith in 1696. In 1737 he married, at Banff, Jean, eldest daughter of William Urquhart of Meldrum, and by her had three sons and two daughters. He died in Banff on 19 June 1756.

Urquhart, John, Waterton, Aberdeenshire

Urquhart, Dr Patrick, Professor of Medicine, King's College, Aberdeen
Fourth son of Patrick Urquhart of Lethenty, afterwards of Meldrum, and his wife, Lady Margaret Ogilvy, daughter of James, 1st Earl of Airlie. Born in 1641, he married Elizabeth, daughter of Dr Andrew Muir, by whom he had eight children. He died in 1725.

Urquhart, William, Merchant in Fraserburgh

Walker, William, Drummer in Old Aberdeen
Illiterate, and on 25 April 1716 he was a married man of approximately 68 years. (See John Ogilvie, Bursar).

Warrander, Robert, Bursar, King's College, Aberdeen
Student in 1716, who made the proclamation in February 1716 "desiring all persons to come and see the Duke of Brunswick in effigie committed to the flames."

White, The Rev George, Minister of Maryculter
Married Marion Cockburn and had three sons and two daughters. He died in 1724.

Whyte, Andrew, Merchant in Aberdeen
Taxer appointed by the Town of Aberdeen.

Whyte, James, Sen
Jacobite at Fraserburgh where the town was searched for the arms left by Lord Lovat and John Forbes of Culloden. These were delivered to George Keith, younger of Ludquharn.

Wilson, George, of Finzeauch
Son of George Wilson of Finzeauch, Burgess of Aberdeen, and Christian Robertson, his wife, he was born in 1659. He married Elizabeth Colinson, and had four sons and five daughters. He died 4 June 1725, aged 66.

JACOBITES OF 1745
NORTH EAST SCOTLAND

Frances McDonnell

Illustration: "Old Gilenbucket"
      George Gordon of Glenbucket

JACOBITES OF 1745
NORTH EAST SCOTLAND

The Sixteenth of April 1996 marks the 250th anniversary of the Battle of Culloden and the end of Jacobite aspirations. The Jacobites were followers of the House of Stuart who, on a number of occasions, attempted to regain the throne of Great Britain from the House of Hanover. In 1745, Charles Edward Stuart (Bonnie Prince Charlie) landed on the island of Eriskay, and rallied his supporters at Glenfinnan on 19 August that year. His purpose was to oust George II, the German whose family had been invited to rule Great Britain to maintain Protestant supremacy. After initial successes over Hanovarian defences as far south as Derby, the Prince failed to persuade enough English Jacobites to join him, which lead to a general demoralisation of an already homesick army. The Jacobites were forced back north, and the final battle of the campaign was fought on the field of Culloden, on the outskirts of Inverness.

Many natural supporters of the Prince came from the Catholic Highlands, but a significant number of Scottish Jacobites were to be found in the North East. This conservative area with its largely Episcopalian landowners maintained its allegiance to the House of Stuart, and this book identifies many of them. Not all supporters were, however, voluntary, many being forced out by their feudal superiors. Many more claimed to have been forced out in an attempt to regain their freedom from imprisonment after Culloden. The following pages give a sometimes graphic description of the sufferings endured by those who were in hiding after the battle, and those who were captured, imprisoned, executed or transported. There are also some physical descriptions of ordinary soldiers who, in the process of being transported, were captured by a French privateer and regained their freedom courtesy of the French on the Caribbean island of Martinique.

After Culloden, many estates were confiscated, and houses raised to the ground. Those who could afford to, escaped to France where they found refuge with their allies, returning after a general amnestice two years later. The more prominent Jacobites who were denied amnesty either stayed where they were, or came home and continued to attempt to evade capture.

Frances McDonnell

BIBLIOGRAPHY

Goren Behre, Goteborg 1982, *Goteborg, Skottland Och Vackre Prinsen*
David Dobson, Genealogical Publishing Co Inc, Baltimore 1989, *The Original Scots Colonists of Early America 1612-1783*
Scottish History Society, Edinburgh, 1929, *Prisoners of the '45, Vol I-III*
Scottish History Society *List of Persons concerned in the Rebellion 1745-46*
Alistair and Henrietta Taylor, *Aberdeenshire and Banffshire in the Forty-Five*, Milne and Hutchison, Aberdeen, 1928
Historic Buildings and Monuments Commission for England, 1984, *List of Prisoners from the Jacobite rebellion 1745, kept in the powder magazines, Tilbury Fort 1746/50*

JACOBITES OF 1745
North East Scotland

Abercromby, James Farmer from Skeith, Banff.   Captain   Prisoner at Carlisle.   Married to Elspeth Ord, daughter of a merchant in Cullen

Aberdeen, James Labourer, Newton, Cruden. Joined after Battle of Preston

Aberdeen, William Merchant, Old Aberdeen.   Vintner in Old Aberdeen and Old Machar.   Acted as Quartermaster.   Murdered in Inverness by English soldiers on the day of the battle of Culloden, as he lay ill in bed in the widow Davidson's house.   His throat was cut   His widow was Ann Dalgarno.

Aberdour, James Brazier, Old Aberdeen   Assisted in uplifting money for the Prince in Old Aberdeen.

Abernethie, George Merchant and Magistrate, Banff   Captain   Prisoner at Carlisle.

Abernethie, John Tanner, Strathbogie   Hired out by the inhabitants, who were forced by John Gordon of Avochie.   Lurking after Culloden

Abernethie, John Overseer of the Highways, Tyrie, Aberdeenshire.

Abernethy, Alexander A farmer in Tipperty, Banff   Also described as a surgeon, with wife and four young children.   Taken prisoner at Carlisle, he was condemned to hang, was reprieved for a time, during which he fell sick and died

Abernethy, George A merchant and Magistrate at Banff, assumed to be brother to James Abernethy of Mayen   Described as cheerful, good-natured and agreeable, he was about 45 years at the time, and a very reluctant rebel   Married to Elizabeth Forbes, daughter of John Forbes of Boyndlie.   He died of consumption on 27 April 1747, and was buried in the churchyard of St Margaret's, Westminster

Adam, James Gardener, Aberdeen.   Carried arms, but deserted and joined HRH the Duke at Culloden.

Adam, John Coal Driver, Aberdeen.   Prisoner in Aberdeen

Adamson, James Gardener at Drum.   He survived the uprising, and is said to have profited from it in spoil

Adamson, William Labourer, Cowlie, Monymusk   Survived Culloden, lurking.

Addison, George Bowman of Aberdeen, in Pitsligo's Horse

Agevy, John Of Aberdeen   Of Farquharson's Regiment, prisoner at Tilbury.

Airth, John Aberdeen.   Prisoner at Culloden

Aitken, Andrew Prisoner in Aberdeen from 22 Jul 1746 to 28 Apr 1747

Alexander, Cosmo John Son of John Alexander, Painter, he himself was a "picture drawer, Aberdeen" He was born in 1724 He visited America after 1766, where he painted portraits at Rhode Island, and then returned to Edinburgh Said to have died in 1772

Alexander, George Glover, Spittall, Old Aberdeen Ensign Lurking after Rising

Alexander, John Painter, born about 1690 Grandson of George Jamesone "The Scottish Vandyck," whose daughter Marjory married John Alexander, Advocate, Edinburgh He married and had at least one son. Cosmo John Said to have died 1760

Allan, James Town Cadie, Aberdeen Carried arms at Inverurie and Culloden

Allan, John Farmer, Moss-side, Banff Private man hired out

Allan, Robert Servant, Old Aberdeen Survived Culloden, prisoner in Old Aberdeen

Allanoch, John Merchant, Clashmore, Banffshire

Allen, James Town Cadie, Aberdeen Imprisoned in Aberdeen for being concerned in Rising at Inverury and Culloden

Anderson, Alexander Servant, Knockiemill, Banff Private man Lurking after Culloden

Anderson, Alexander Servant, Upper Dallalchy, Banffshire A sergeant and enlisted man Prisoner

Anderson, Alexander, of Tynet Lurking after Culloden

Anderson, Charles Merchant, Old Meldrum Collected levy money

Anderson, James Barber, Old Aberdeen With the army from the beginning

Anderson, James Resident in Bellie, Morayshire Transported April 1747

Anderson, James Merchant, Upper Dalachie, Banff Ensign and very active

Anderson, John Craighead, Marnoch, Banffshire Gentleman, Ensign Lurking after Culloden

Anderson, John Born 1729 Gardener, Aberdeen 5ft 2ins, dark hair, well made Transported 5 May 1747 from Liverpool to Leeward Islands in *Veteran*, but the ship was attacked off Antigua by a French privateer from Martinique The Governor of Martinique refused English demands to hand the prisoners back, and granted the request of 10 to be sent to France possibly to negotiate for others

Anderson, John Banff Servant to Mr Forbes, prisoner in Tilbury

Anderson, John, yr of Greens Eldest son of John Anderson and his wife, Margaret Forbes, only daughter and heiress of James Forbes of Greens, a family which had owned that property for 100 years He was 25 years old at the Rising He died, unmarried, 4 Oct 1767 aged 47, and was succeeded by his sister, Margaret

Anderson, William Vintner, Old Aberdeen

Andrew, William Banff Prisoner in Inverness

Angus, George Tailor of Longside, Buchan A prisoner at Peterhead, 5 June 1746, released 26 August 1746

Angus, William Labourer, Newton of Cruden Joined after Preston

Angus, William Old Meldrum

Annan (or Annand), Alexander Born 1728. Butcher, Aberdeen Prisoner in Aberdeen. Transported 24 Feb 1747 from Liverpool to Virginia in *Gildart*, arrived Port North Potomac, Maryland, 5 Aug 1747

Annand, James Aberdeen. Duke of Perth's Regiment, in Carlisle garrison

Arbuthnot, John Born 1684 Tailor, of Aberdeen Carlisle garrison Transported 22 April 1747 from Liverpool to Virginia in *Johnson*, arrived Port North Potomac, Maryland, 5 Aug 1747

Arbuthnot, Thomas Sailor, Peterhead

Arbuthnot, Thomas, sen Merchant in Peterhead Eldest son of Nathaniel Arbuthnot in Auchlee, Longside, and Elspeth Duncan his wife Assisted the Old Chevalier on his landing at Peterhead on 25 Dec 1715, and arranged for his being safely lodged in the Longate Aged 64 in 1745 He married Christian Young, daughter of William Young, merchant, Peterhead, and had two sons, James and Thomas, and five daughters. He died on 24 Mar 1762, aged 81, and his wife on 8 Feb 1740, aged 55

Arbuthnot, Thomas, yr Second son of Baillie Thomas Arbuthnot He fought as a Lieutenant at Culloden, afterwards escaping to France and subsequently commanded his own ship in the West Indian and American trade. He married his cousin, Margaret Arbuthnot, eldest daughter of James Arbuthnot of Rora, by whom he had three sons and two daughters Died at Peterhead 1 Dec 1773, aged 46

Auld, Janet Prisoner in Tolbooth, Aberdeen

Auld, William Huxter, Aberdeen Carried arms at Inverury and Culloden Prisoner at Aberdeen.

Bagrie, William Labourer, Gateside, Cruden Joined after Falkirk

Bain, George Born 21 June 1722, son of Alexander Bain, Kemnay, Aberdeenshire Labourer Aberdeen, 5ft 5 5ins, black hair, swarthy Transported 5 May 1747 from Liverpool on the *Vetaran*, but the ship was attacked off Antigua by a French privateer from Martinique The Governor of Martinique refused English demands to hand the prisoners back, and granted the request of 10 to be sent to France possibly to negotiate for others.

Bain, John, yr Glenconglass, Banffshire Forced to serve, submitted to King's mercy.

Bain-Stewart, Archibald Delavorar, Banffshire. Forced to serve

Baird, William, of Auchmedden Born in 1701 and married in 1721, Anne, daughter of William Duff of Dipple. Died in 1775, aged 74, and his wife died in 1773. They had six sons and four daughters, all of whom died without issue except Henrietta, the youngest, who married Francis Fraser of Dindrack, Aberdeenshire.

Baird, William Born 6 June 1729, St Nicholas, Aberdeen, son of William Baird and Janet Brown. Wool Merchant and Silk Dyer, Aberdeen The first wool merchant in Aberdeen to introduce the use of machinery in his business. Transported 24 Feb 1747 from Liverpool to Virginia in *Gildart*, arrived Port North Potomac, Maryland, 5 Aug 1747.

Jacobites of North East Scotland 1745

Bannerman, Sir Alexander, Bart. of Elsick   Son of Sir Alexander Bannerman 2nd Baronet and his wife, Isabella, daughter of Sir Alexander Macdonald of Sleat   He succeeded his father in 1742 and married Isabella, heiress of the Trotters of Horsley, Yorkshire   He had two sons and one daughter   He died in 1747 in Paris

Barclay, Gilbert Cruden, Aberdeenshire

Barclay, John Shoemaker, Fochabers, Moray   Lurking after Culloden

Barclay, Robert Merchant, Aberdeen   In the Prince's Life Guards   Took refuge in Sweden after Culloden

Barclay, William Cabinetmaker, Aberdeen   Carlisle garrison, pardoned on enlistment

Baxter, George Aberdeen   Prisoner there

Baxter, Robert Labourer, Netherhaugh, Strachan, Kincardine   Was at Falkirk, but said to be forced out

Bean, George Writer in Aberdeen   Prisoner there

Begg, ... Servant to Glenbucket   Hid Glenbucket's flintlock in a Moss, it is now in the Museum at Clova

Begg, Alexander Tanner, Akinboe, Aberdeenshire   Hired out

Bell, David Weaver, Aberdeen

Bennagagh, John Banffshire   Prisoner at Carlisle

Bennet, Robert Merchant, Fochabers, Moray   Lurking after Culloden

Bettie, Alexander Labourer, Rothney, Premnay

Beverley, John Aberdeen   Prisoner at Culloden   Transported 22 April 1747 from Liverpool to Virginia in *Johnson*, arrived Port Oxford, Maryland 5 Aug 1747

Beverley, John Aberdeen   Transported 22 April 1747 from Liverpool to Virginia in *Johnson*, arrived Port Oxford, Maryland, 5 Aug 1747

Bickley, James Miller's apprentice, Miln of Turriff, Banff   Lurking after Culloden

Binnachie, John Weaver, Bellandy, Glenrinnes

Birse, William Labourer, Carlaurg, Birse, Deeside   At Falkirk battle, said to be forced out

Bisset, James Servant to John Downie, Little Clinarty, Newhills   At Falkirk and Culloden, lurking

Bowie, James Brewer and Malster, Cullen, Banff   At the plundering of Cullen House   Lurking after Culloden

Bowie, James Souie, Glenlivet

Bowie (or Bouie), John Born 1733, Servant, Aberdeen   Aged 14, nut brown, 5ft lively   Transported 5 May 1747 from Liverpool to Leeward Islands in *Veteran*, but the ship was attacked off Antigua by a French privateer from Martinique   The Governor of Martinique refused English demands to hand the prisoners back, and granted the request of 10 to be sent to France possibly to negotiate for others

Bowie, Robert Parkmore, Banffshire

Bowie, Robert Born 1733, servant   Resident in Strathbogie, Aberdeenshire   Transported 22 April 1747 from Liverpool to Virginia in *Johnson*, arrived Port Oxford, Maryland, 5 Aug 1747

Bowman, James Farmer, Todlehills, Ellon   Joined after Falkirk

4

Bowman, James Householder, Portsoy, Banff.

Brady, William Labourer, Rathven. Carlisle garrison.

Brand, Robert Labourer, Banchory   At Culloden.

Brander, James Banff.   Died on *Thane of Fife* transport ship to London, Sept 1746.

Breber-Mackinteer, Angus Auchlanie   Very active in plundering

Brebner, George Labourer, Aberdeen

Bredy, John Labourer, Old Machar, Aberdeen.   At Culloden

Bremner, George Wright and servant, Carnousie   Lurking after Culloden

Bremner, George Shoemaker, Fochabers, Moray   Lurking after Culloden

Bremner, Robert Weaver, Fochabers, Moray   Lurking after Culloden

Bremner, Walter Pedlar, Gilston, Aberdeen.

Bridgefoord, Magnus Upper Mains of Blairydroyne, Durris, Aberdeenshire   At Culloden

Brodie, William, in Cottoun, Glenbucket Eldest son of Alastair Brodie and his wife, Jean Morris.   He married on 13 Jul 1738 Jean Brebner, and left children.   He died at Dalfrankie, Glenbucket in 1776

Broun, Joseph Born, 1731, tailor, Banff.   Transported 5 May 1747 from Liverpool to Leeward Islands in *Veteran*, but the ship was attacked off Antigua by a French privateer from Martinique   The Governor of Martinique refused English demands to hand the prisoners back, and granted the request of 10 to be sent to France possibly to negotiate for others

Broun, William Servant, Carnousie, Wauk Miln, Banff   Lurking after Culloden.

Brown, John Carnousie

Brown, John Ballindouan   Forced out and deserted

Brown, Joseph Aged 16, tailor, Banff   5ft 6ins, dark complexion, well made, healthy   Transported 5 May 1747 from Liverpool to Leeward Islands in *Veteran*, but the ship was attacked off Antigua by a French privateer from Martinique   The Governor of Martinique refused English demands to hand the prisoners back, and granted the request of 10 to be sent to France possibly to negotiate for others

Bruce, John Aberdeen.   Prisoner there.

Bruce, Robert Labourer, Old Meldrum.

Buchan, George Labourer, Old Meldrum

Buchan, James Labourer, Leys, Ellon

Buchan, John Labourer, Hillhead of Cruden   Joined after Falkirk battle

Burboy, John Cordwainer, Strathbogie.

Burnet, John Esq. junior of Campfield, Kincardine.   Eldest son of William Burnet of Campfield, and Anne, daughter of Sir John Guthrie of King Edward, he was baptised in 1716   He was a young man in the '45 and the only thoroughly trained gunner officer.   He married in 1743 a daughter of Lumsden of Cushny, and had four daughters.   Taken prisoner at Carlisle, he almost died in Newgate, but later became a successful merchant in Holland.

Burnet, William Labourer, Collonach, Strachan, Drumoak, Kincardineshire   Was at Falkirk and Culloden

Bygowan, George Servant, Kintore, Aberdeen   Hired out
Byres, Patrick (or Peter), of Tonley Second and only surviving son of
Robert Byres and his wife, Jean Sandilands, daughter of Patrick
Sandilands of Aberdeen, born 13 May 1713   About the time of his
birth, his father was accidentally drowned in Dublin Bay, and the
widow soon after returned with her children to Aberdeenshire, where,
in 1718 she bought Tonley   Married in 1733, Janet, daughter of
James Moir, 3rd of Stoneywood, and his second wife, Jean Abernethy,
of Mayen   They had four sons and three daughters   Lurking after
Rising, he died at Tonley, 3 Sept 1817, in his 84th year
Calder, John A young servant, Burnhead, Birse, Aberdeenshire   At
Culloden, but said to be forced out
Calder, Robert Sailor, Aberdeen   Carried arms
Cameron, Alexander Born 1727, resident in Nairn   Transported 31 March
1747 from Tilbury to Barbados in *Frere*
Cameron, John Croftbain, Banffshire
Cameron, John Miller in Ruthven of Kirkmichael
Campbell, Alexander Labourer, Clatt or Claddie, Aberdeenshire
Transported 22 April 1747 from Liverpool to Virginia in *Johnson*,
arrived Port Oxford, Maryland, 5 Aug 1747
Campbell, Angus Carrier, Banff
Campbell, Donald Servant to Pitfoddels   Laid down his arms
Campbell, Donald Fodderletter   Carried arms but submitted himself
Campbell, John Fodderletter
Campbell, John Aberdeen   Prisoner at Musselburgh, escaped
Carr, Nicholas Piper Huntly   Carlisle garrison, acquitted
Cato, James House carpenter, Fraserburgh
Cattanach, Andrew Banff, prisoner after Culloden
Cattanach, Duncan Braes of Mar
Catto, Alexander Weaver in Aberdeen
Chalmers, George Salmon fisher, Don Bridge, Aberdeen   At Falkirk and
Culloden   Survived and lurking after the Rising
Chalmers, Isobel Born 1722, knitter of Aberdeen or The Mearns   5ft 7ins,
black hair tall and slender   Followed Glengarry's Regiment, taken at
Carlisle   Transported 5 May 1747 from Liverpool to Leeward Islands
in *Veteran* but the ship was attacked off Antigua by a French privateer
from Martinique   The Governor of Martinique refused English
demands to hand the prisoners back, and granted the request of 10 to
be sent to France possibly to negotiate for others
Chalmers, John Farmer, Methlick   Was at Inverurie Skirmish and assisted
in taking prisoners there, went to the Supervisor's room with three
armed men in quest of books relating to revenue
Chalmers, William Baker, of Fraserburgh   Concerned in apprehending
Captain Grant on his way to join Lord Loudoun at Inverness
Chape (or Chapp), James Born 1726, smith at St Marnoch Church,
Banffshire   Prisoner in Edinburgh   Transported 24 Feb 1747 from
Liverpool in *Gildart*, arr Port North Potomac, Maryland 5 Aug 1747

Chapman, James Gardener, Durn, Banffshire. Transported 22 April 1747 from Liverpool to Virginia in *Johnson*, arrived Port Oxford, Maryland, 5 Aug 1747.

Chapman, John Servant to Sir William Gordon of Park

Chapman, William Pedlar, Aberdeenshire, 32 years old, 5ft 4ins, pale complexion, healthy. Transported 5 May 1747 from Liverpool to Leeward Islands in *Veteran*, but the ship was attacked off Antigua by a French privateer from Martinique. The Governor of Martinique refused English demands to hand the prisoners back, and granted the request of 10 to be sent to France possibly to negotiate for others

Charles, James Tailor in Aberdeen

Chein, George Sailor, Fraserburgh

Chicad, William Banff.

Chivas, John Labourer, Rothney, Premnay

Christie, Alexander Aged 21, Aberdeen   Prisoner in Inverness

Christie, Alexander Aged 19, Aberdeen   Prisoner in Inverness

Christie, David Aged 21, Aberdeen   Prisoner in Inverness

Christy, Patrick Farmer, Corsairtly, Banffshire   Sergeant   Lurking after Culloden.

Christy, William Shipmaster, Fraserburgh   Concerned in apprehending Captain Grant.

Clapperton, Thomas Weaver, Fochabers, Banffshire   Transported 22 April 1747 from Liverpool to Virginia in *Johnson*, arrived Port Oxford, Maryland, 5 Aug 1747

Clapperton, William Born 1734, son of Thomas Clapperton   A ploughboy of 13, in Glenbucket's regiment   Pardoned because of his youth, he was nevertheless transported on *Veteran* on 5 May 1747 from Liverpool, but the ship was attacked off Antigua by a French privateer from Martinique   The Governor of Martinique refused English demands to hand the prisoners back, and granted the request of 10 to be sent to France possibly to negotiate for others

Clark, Alexander Aberdeen at Culloden

Clark, Alexander Dyster, Fochabers, Moray   Prisoner

Clark, Andrew Labourer, Wester Colarly, Echt   At Falkirk and Culloden

Clark, James Chapman, Slains   Prisoner at Stirling, liberated

Clark, John Ruthven in Kirkmichael   Quartermaster, and very active

Clark, William Labourer, Little Artrachy, Cruden   Joined after Preston

Clavering, Elizabeth Born 1725, seamstress, Banff, 22 years old, 5ft, brown hair, thin. Transported 5 May 1747 from Liverpool to Leeward Islands in *Veteran*, but the ship was attacked off Antigua by a French privateer from Martinique   The Governor of Martinique refused English demands to hand the prisoners back, and granted the request of 10 to be sent to France possibly to negotiate for others.

Clows, Robert Banchory.

Coats, William Born 1692.   Labourer, Aberdeenshire.   5ft 3ins, dark hair, shot in right shoulder   Transported 5 May 1747 from Liverpool to Leeward Islands in *Veteran*, but the ship was attacked off Antigua by a French privateer from Martinique.   The Governor of Martinique refused English demands to hand the prisoners back, and granted the request of 10 to be sent to France possibly to negotiate for others

Collie, George Pitfoddels

Colquhoun, Archibald Aberdeen   Prisoner at Culloden

Cormack, John Servant to Dorlaithers, Aberdeen   Recruited men

Coutts, David, jun Wright, Aberdeen   At Falkirk and Culloden

Coutts, James Banchory, Upper Banchory, Aberdeenshire   A poor man

Coutts, John Baker's apprentice, Aberdeen   Was one of the mob who broke the Town's drum when solemnising the Prince of Wales' birthday

Coutts, Peter, Merchant, Aberdeen   Possibly more a talker than a soldier Involved in the Inverury skirmish

Coutts, William Aberdeen   Monaltrie's Regiment

Coutts, William Boatman in Torry, Nigg   Prisoner in Aberdeen

Coutts, William Inverourie, Banffshire

Cowie, Alexander Weaver, Fochabers, Moray   Killed at Culloden

Craig, Alexander Aberdeen   In prison there

Craig, Alexander Merchant, Rosehearty   Joined at Edinburgh, worth money

Craig, George Wright, Loanhead, Old Machar   At Culloden

Crawford, Alexander Of the parish of Gamrie   A rebel soldier, died at Nethermill Friday 28 March 1746, and was buried at Essil

Crawford, Patrick Vintner at Don Bridge   Prisoner in Aberdeen

Crichton, James, of Auchingoul   Second son of James Crichton of Auchingoul who married Margaret Gordon   The elder son appears to have been disinherited, and the father died in 1744   He escaped abroad and lived in France   He died in poverty at Paris in 1769

Cristal, David Old Aberdeen, Old Machar   Assisted in unloading the Spanish ship at Peterhead   Survived the Rising

Cristal, John Wright Aberdeen   Assisted in unloading the Spanish ship at Peterhead   Was concerned in a mob at Old Aberdeen, apprehended and admitted to bail   Lurking after Battle of Culloden

Cruickshank, Hector Delavorar

Cruickshank, James Labourer, Miln of Bonnytoun, Rayne

Cruickshank, Dr John Surgeon, Fraserburgh   Joined the army at Edinburgh   prisoner in Aberdeen

Cruickshank, John Delavorar   A deserter

Cruickshank, John Weaver   A prisoner in the Tolbooth, Aberdeen

Cruickshank, John Born 1733   Herdsman, Aberdeen, aged 14, 5ft, fair complexion, healthy   Carlisle garrison   Transported 5 May 1747 from Liverpool to Leeward Islands in *Veteran*, but the ship was attacked off Antigua by a French privateer from Martinique   The Governor of Martinique refused English demands to hand the prisoners back, and granted the request of 10 to be sent to France possibly to negotiate for others

Cruickshank, Robert Delavorar   Forced out, but submitted himself

Cruickshank, Robert Badinglashean, Ballindalloch

Cumine, Alexander Younger brother of Charles Cumine (or Cumming) of Kininmonth, described as a farmer in Meikle Crichie, Old Deer. Third son of John Cumine of Kininmonth. Taken prisoner at Culloden and shipped to Tilbury. He returned and is buried with his brother

Cumine (or Cumming), Charles, of Kininmonth Eldest son of John Cumine, 2nd of Kininmonth, and Mary Keith, his wife, of the Marischal family He had three brothers. Married before 1740 the Hon Sophia, daughter of 15th Lord Forbes, who died aged 75 in 1790 After Culloden he went into hiding, but through his wife's influence he secured a pardon (she was presented to George II and described her husband as 'a fool'.) He lived for 18 years after Culloden, but was uncomfortable at home while others were being hunted about the country. He died in 1764 aged 57.

Cumine, William, of Pitullie Eldest son of George Cumine, 2nd of Pitullie by his first wife Jean, daughter of Captain Robert Urquhart of Burdsyards (now Sandquhar), Forres, born in 1721 By his first wife he had four sons and two daughters, and in 1728 he married Christian, daughter of Sir John Guthrie of Ludquharn, by whom he had 17 children. In 1752 he married Jean, daughter of William Moir of Lonmay, and had an additional 9 children Died Edinburgh in 1790

Cumming, David Servant, Aberdeen Killed at Culloden

Cumming, Jane Resident of Alvie, Morayshire Transported 22 April 1747 from Liverpool to Virginia in *Johnson*, arrived Port Oxford, Maryland 5 Aug 1747.

Cumming, John Collector of Excise at Aberdeen Dismissed from his post for being concerned in the Rising

Cumming, John Tombae. An officer, but deserted and submitted himself

Cumming, Lauchlan Tomintoul.

Dalgarno, John Merchant, Auchmunzle, New Deer Recruited men

Dalgetty, John Tidesman, Aberdeen Dismissed from his post for being concerned in the Rising

Daniel, James Aberdeen. Carlisle garrison

Davidson, Alexander Born 1720, resident of Charton, Aberdeenshire Prisoner at Culloden. Transported 31 Mar 1747 from London to Barbados in *Frere*.

Davidson, Andrew Labourer, Hill of Tillycairn, Clunie.

Davidson, George Glenconglass

Davidson, James Aged 14. Servant to Gordon of Carnousie "a very wicked boy." Released.

Davidson, James Aberdeen. Carlisle garrison.

Davidson, John Inchnacape. Compelled to carry arms, submitted himself

Davidson, John Auchriachan, Tomintoul

Davidson, John Prisoner at Culloden. Deserted from Guise's Regiment

Davidson, Peter Servant, Balnacraig, Aboyne. Carried arms in England, Falkirk and Culloden.

Davidson, William Tailor, Turriff. Returned to the country, lurking after Culloden.

Davidson, William Aberdeen. Carlisle garrison.

Dawson, James Wright, Kinminity, Banff   Hired out   Lurking after Culloden

Deans, Andrew Labourer, Hill of Tillycairn, Clunie   Lurking after Culloden

Decorm, Alexander, jun Servant, Aberdeen   Lieutenant   Lurking after Culloden

Decorm, Alexander, sen Wright, Aberdeen   Tidesman for the Jacobites, Port of Aberdeen

Derg, Angus Tombreck of Fodderletter

Dick, Alexander Labourer, Turnilove, Cruden

Dick, David Born 1725, shoemaker   Transported 24 Feb 1747 from Liverpool to Virginia in *Gildart*, arrived Port North Potomac, Maryland 5 Aug 1747

Dickie, Margaret Of the parish of Bellie, Banffshire   Prisoner in Lancaster Gaol, she was pardoned 24 March 1747

Dirom, Alexander, sen Writer and Collector of Taxes in Aberdeen, he discreetly disappeared in November 1756

Dirom, Alexander, jun Aberdeen   Son of Alexander Dirom, sen, born in 1725   Believed to be the much respected Provost of Banff

Donald, James Servant to Pitfoddels

Donald, James Aged 20, tailor, Mearnshire, 5ft 7 5ins, brown hair, brown complexion well made   Transported 5 May 1747 from Liverpool to Leeward Islands in *Veteran*, but the ship was attacked off Antigua by a French privateer from Martinique   The Governor of Martinique refused English demands to hand the prisoners back, and granted the request of 10 to be sent to France possibly to negotiate for others

Donaldson, Alexander Born 1707, labourer, resident in Banff   Transported 1747

Donaldson, James Servant to Hay of Rannes (or Ranass, Banffshire)   Prisoner at Inverness   Born 1722   Transported 1747 from Tilbury

Douglas, Alexander Cobleheugh, Banchory, Kincardineshire   Killed at Culloden

Douglas, John A cottar, Glass Well, Banchory   At Inverurie and Culloden

Douglas, John, of Fechil, Ellon Son of Sylvester Douglas of Whiteriggs, Kincardineshire, and married, first Elizabeth, daughter of Charles Maitland of Pitrichie, and after her death, Margaret, daughter of James Gordon MD of Fechil and his wife, Margaret Baird, daughter of James Baird of Auchmedden   By his second wife he had a son, Sylvester born 1743 and a daughter, Katherine   His third wife was Margaret, daughter of Thomas Forbes of Echt   He died 28 Apr 1762 aged 47

Douglas, Samuel Late Supervisor of Excise, Forres   Killed

Douglass, Patrick Banffshire   Carlisle garrison

Downie, John Farmer, Little Clinarty, Newhills   Lieutenant, and lurking after Culloden

Drysdale, Neil or Nathaniel   An Aberdeen schoolboy of fourteen, he was taken prisoner after Culloden and sent to London on the *Greyhound*   He made himself so useful to the officers when it was attacked by a French privateer off Loch Moidart and many of the crew were sick, that on arrival in London he was discharged without trial

Duff, James Third surviving son of Alexander Duff, 1st of Hatton   He was born in 1729.   At 16 he was brought back after a skirmish at Inverurie, and owing to his youth and the family interest the matter was hushed up   In 1761 he was appointed Sheriff Clerk of Banff, and held the office for 40 years.   Twice married, firstly to Helen, daughter of George Skene of Rubislaw, who bore him a daughter, Helen, and two sons, Alexander and George,   secondly to Margaret, daughter of James Dunbar of Kincorth, and by her had thirteen children   Died in 1804, aged 75
Duff, John Baker, Banff
Duff, William Eldest son of Lord Braco, born in 1724   Described as "an abandoned wretch, nothing can ever be expected from him," by his father, he died in 1753 and was buried at night (to avoid the seizure of his body for debt!) in St Margaret's Church, Westminster
Duffus, Alexander Messenger, Fochabers, Moray   Lurking after Culloden
Duguid, George Merchant, Aberdeen, "had to find security for good behaviour "
Duguid, Patrick (or Peter), of Auchinhove, Lumphanan Son of Robert Duguid of Auchinhove and his wife, Teresa, third daughter of Patrick, Count Leslie of Balquhain, born in 1700   In 1731 he married Isabella Dickson, by whom he had three sons and one daughter, who all died in infancy.   He married, secondly, in 1740, Amelia, daughter of John Irvine of Kincausie, by whom he had 11 children, the fourth son, John, ultimately succeeding him.   He married for a third time in 1773, Eliza Grant, his cousin   Lurking near own house after Culloden   Died 11 Apr 1777, aged 76.
Duguid, Peter Vintner, Old Meldrum
Dunbar, James Born 1730, labourer, Morayshire   Transported 5 May 1747 from Liverpool to Leeward Islands in *Veteran*, but the ship was attacked off Antigua by a French privateer from Martinique   The Governor of Martinique refused English demands to hand the prisoners back, and granted the request of 10 to be sent to France possibly to negotiate for others.
Dunbar, Michael He was a well-known character in the Strathdon district where he was a terror to the countryside, being a noted thief, robber and, when driven to it, a murderer.   He survived the Rising and is said to have been over 100 years when he died
Dunbar, Sir William of Durn Eldest son of Sir James Dunbar and his wife, Margaret, daughter of Sir James Baird of Auchmedden   Married Clementina, daughter of Sir James Grant of Grant in 1737, and had three sons and four daughters.   He married for a second time, in 1765, Jane Bartlett of Banff, by whom he had no male issue   He died in Banff on 28 Jan 1786.
Duncan, George Servant, Fochabers, Moray.   Lurking after Culloden.
Duncan, James Servant, Turriff.   Lurking after Culloden.
Duncan, John White Fisher in Footdee, in prison in Aberdeen.
Duncan, John Prisoner at Culloden, deserted, of Aberdeen.

11

Duncan, Thomas Tillygarmouth, Aberdeenshire   At Falkirk, said to be
    forced out
Dunn, James Labourer, Calton of Cockardy, Kincardineshire   At Culloden
Dunn, John Labourer, Calton of Cockardy
Dunnon, John Banff
Durrar, William Born 1717, servant, Ashdale, Aberdeenshire   Prisoner at
    Culloden Transported 20 March 1747 from Tilbury
Durrie, Alexander Tide-waiter in Aberdeen, prisoner there
Durward, George Labourer, Bauds, Aboyne   At Falkirk
Durward, George Labourer, Band, Birss, Aberdeenshire   At Falkirk, but
    said to be forced out
Durward, John Saddler, Old Meldrum   At Inverurie
Durward, Malcolm, of Mulloch, Aberdeenshire   He was present at
    Culloden and two of his brothers were killed by his side
Durward, Robert Labourer, Bauds, Aboyne
Durward, Robert Labourer, Band, Birss, Aberdeenshire   At Falkirk, but
    said to be forced out
Dyce, James Of Aberdeen In French picquets, prisoner at Culloden
Easson, John A cottar, Lorichmore, Strachan, Kincardineshire   At
    Culloden
Easson, Robert Labourer, Formiston, Aboyne   At Falkirk and Culloden,
    and very active plundering
Edinson, William Banffshire
Edward, Francis Servant to William Booth, Aberdeen
Edward, Michael Blacksmith, Old Machar, Old Aberdeen
Edward, William Shoemaker, Old Aberdeen   Assisted in unloading the
    Spanish ship, was apprehended but admitted to bail
Egon (or Egor), John Crathie   At Culloden   Died at Tilbury Fort
Elder, John Servant to Sir William Gordon of Park   Lurking after Culloden
Elphinstone, Henry, sen Described as a merchant in Aberdeen, and a
    discharged land waiter, he had a son, John, born in 1723   Prisoner in
    Edinburgh
Elphinstone, Henry, jun Went to Carlisle with the rebels, from whence he
    deserted   In the Register Book of St Paul's Episcopal Chapel,
    Aberdeen dated 19 July 1747, there is this entry, "Hary Elphinstone,
    junior shipmaster and Jean Elphinstone had a daughter Mary "
Elphinstone, William Servant to Dr Gregory, prisoner in Aberdeen
Ewing, Charles Labourer, Charlestown, Aboyne   At Falkirk and Culloden,
    and very active plundering   Lurking after Culloden
Ewing, Peter Labourer, Croft, Glentanner   At Falkirk, and nowhere else
Ewing, Robert Soldier and deserter, Charlestown, Aboyne   At Falkirk and
    killed at Culloden
Falconer, Alexander Sailor, Fraserburgh
Falconer, William Prisoner at Culloden
Farquhar, Francis Servant, Finzean, Deeside
Farquhar, James Farmer, Burnside, Banff   Lurking after Culloden

Farquhar, John Groom to John Murray of Broughton. Had been ostler at the Red Lion in Edinburgh, but said to be born in Banffshire Captured and transported to London, his ultimate fate is not known

Farquhar, William Prisoner in Aberdeen, labourer in Glasgowego

Farquharson, Andrew Lived at Balintomb, Kirkmichael, and was an unwilling participant

Farquharson, Anne Wife of Aeneas Mackintosh, 22nd Laird of Mackintosh Daughter of James, 9th Laird of Invercauld and Margaret Muray, born in Aberdeenshire. Her husband was firmly on the Government side, and was taken prisoner by the Jacobites at Dornoch The Prince had the happy idea of sending him into the custody of "Colonel Anne." She was captured after Culloden, but set free after six weeks confinement in Inverness She died in 1757

Farquharson, Rev Charles Youngest son of Lewis Farquharson of Acuhindryne and his wife, Margaret Farquharson of Allanaquoich, born in 1713 He became a Jesuit priest, and was a renowned physician Died at Ardearg, 30 Nov 1799, aged 86

Farquharson, Charles Third son of Andrew Farquharson of Allargue and Barbara Stewart of Aucholzie, born in 1719. He lived at Cluny-on-the-Dee, opposite Invercauld House until his death, on 21 Jan 1795

Farquharson, Charles, in Drumnapark of Monaltrie Son of Donald of the Auchriachan branch of Farquharsons, his mother being a daughter of James Coutts, Rifantrach Married Barbara, eldest daughter and co-heiress of Charles Farquharson, of first Monaltrie family They had 10 sons and 1 daughter between 1733 and 1751

Farquharson, Charles Farmer, Drumnopark, Glenmuck, Aberdeenshire Ensign Lurking after Culloden

Farquharson, Cosmo, in Tombae Son of Gregor Farquharson, named after his father's pupil and patron, Cosmo, Duke of Gordon Thought to have escaped after Culloden

Farquharson, Donald, of Auchriachan Eldest son of Robert Farquharson of Auchriachan He married Mary, eldest daughter of William Burnet of Campfield and sister of John Burnet, the Jacobite They had 3 sons and 4 daughters Erroneously "reported killed" at Culloden, in November 1746 he was "at home," and later escaped to France where he died before 1756. His wife died on 31 Jan 1795, in her 83rd year

Farquharson, Francis of Monaltrie One of the most important Aberdeenshire Jacobites Second son of Alexander Farquharson of Monaltrie and his wife, Ann Farquharson, daughter of Francis Farquharson of Finzean, born in 1710. He was a prisoner for 20 years, four months and one day, from the battle of Culloden Long after the Rising he married Elizabeth Eyre of Hassop in Derbyshire, who is buried in Durham, where she died in March 1786 They had no children. He brought many improvements to agriculture after rebuilding his house of Monaltrie. He died in 1790.

Farquharson, Francis Farmer, Bogg, Tarland, Aberdeenshire Killed at Culloden.

Farquharson, Francis Servant, Phinzian, Birss, Aberdeenshire At Culloden, but said to be forced out.

Farquharson, Gregor, in Tombae Fourth son of Charles Bui Farquharson, a tenant on the Monaltrie estate, educated at the Scots College in Paris He lived at Glenlivet, married and had children He probably died in captivity

Farquharson, Harry Farmer, Whitehouse Mill, Colston, Aberdeenshire Eldest son of Harry Farquharson of Whitehouse Mill, by his second wife, Elizabeth Harper Killed at Culloden He had married in 1720, Barbara daughter of John Gordon of Hallhead and had four sons, Harry. William, James and Robert, and two daughters

Farquharson, Henry Farmer, Whitehouse Miln, Colston, Aberdeenshire Captain At Falkirk and lurking after Culloden

Farquharson, James, of Balmoral Youngest son by the second marriage of John Farquharson of Inverey and his wife, Marjory Leith, daughter of George Leith of Overhall Married Jean Leith, daughter of William Leith of the Overhall family, probably a first cousin They had no family He died about 1753

Farquharson, James Balmurret, Craigmile, Kincardine At Lt Col, he was in England, wounded at Falkirk and was lurking after Culloden

Farquharson, John, of Allargue Eldest son of Andrew Farquharson of Allargue and his wife, Barbara Strewart, daughter of William Stewart of Aucholzie In 1745 he was 33 years of age, resided at Ellick, Kirkmichael and was married to Anna, daughter of Robert Farquharson of Auchriachan He was the father of six young children Captured at Culloden, he was transported to London on a Government vessel in dreadful conditions After some time in captivity he escaped to France on 21 Apr 1748, and lived for many years in Dunkirk

Farquharson, Rev John Third son of Lewis Farquharson of Auchindryne and Margaret Farquharson of Allanaquoich, born at Braemar in 1699 Arrested with his brother Charles in July 1746, they were confined for a long time on board the *Pamela* at Woolwich, where they were held to be saints They were discharged on condition of "leaving the country" He returned to Scotland in 1773, and died 22 Aug 1782 aged 83

Farquharson, John Farmer, Bogg, Tarland, Aberdeenshire An Ensign at Culloden, and killed there

Farquharson, John Dow Servant in Auchriachan, probably to Donald Farquharson A member of the Farquharson family had a natural son called John Dow

Farquharson, Lewis Farmer, Bog, Tarland Son of Alexander Farquharson of Tullycairn, his mother being a daughter of Peter Gordon of Blelack He had seven sons, named Francis, John, Charles, Robert, Alexander Lewis and Harry Francis, John and Robert were definitely killed at Culloden

Farquharson, Lewis Labourer, Foggyridge, Rayne

Farquharson, Robert, Mill of Auchriachan Of the Auchriachan family, he came safely through the Rising, and in 1755 was living in Glenorchy Married Sophia Macgregor, and had a son called William born in Glenrochy. and a daughter, Janet His wife died May 1769, aged 59

Farquharson, Robert Home given as 'Tullich, Glenmuick'. He was a deserter from the Hanovarian army, and would have been shot if captured. Ensign. Lurking after Culloden

Farquharson, Robert Farmer, Bogg, Tarland, Aberdeenshire Ensign at Culloden and killed there.

Farquharson, Robert Dow Probably servant to John Farquharson of Allargue, and probably a natural son of a member of the family, the cognomen "Dow" being frequently used in such cases

Farquharson, William Son of Lewis Farquharson of Auchindryne and brother of the two Jesuit priests, John and Charles He took possession of Auchindryne after the death of his elder brother, Alistair in 1739. Present at Culloden.

Farquharson, William Farmer, Tarland, probably one of the three brothers of the Tullycairn family who came from Crathie Survived Culloden Transported 31 March 1747 from London to Barbados in *Frere*

Farquharson William Banffshire Prisoner at Culloden

Ferguson, James Tomintoul

Ferguson, James Aberdeen At Culloden

Ferrier, David Labourer, Cothill, Ellon Joined after Falkirk

Ferrier, James Sailor, Fraserburgh.

Fife, William Farmer, Down, Banff A volunteer

Fillan, Alexander Labourer, Kirkton, Aboyne

Findlater, William Shoemaker, Spittal, Old Machar, Aberdeen. Assisted in transporting the Spanish arms from Peterhead Surrendered and admitted to bail.

Findlay, Robert Labouring servant, Balfidie, Birss, Aberdeenshire At Culloden, but said to be forced out

Findlay, William Labourer, Balfidie, Birse

Finlay, Alexander Weaver, Elgin

Finlay, William Croughly, Banffshire.

Fleming, Alexander Born 1727 Horsehirer in Aberdeen Crichton of Auchingoul's Regiment Transported 24 Feb 1747 from Liverpool to Virginia in *Gildart*, arrived Port North Potomac, Maryland 5 Aug 1747

Fleming, Donald Mill of Achdregnie Seen in his wounds after Culloden His house was burnt.

Fleming, Duncan In Auchinloan, Glenmuick, "slain in the battle of Culloden."

Fleming, James Croughly, near Tomintoul.

Fleming, John Servant to Glenbucket, younger. Submitted with his master

Fleming, John Findran, Banffshire Deserted in February 1746

Fleming, Patrick, of Auchintoul, Aberdeenshire From a very old Aberdeenshire family said to have had property since 1411 Survived Culloden by feigning death, despite having a Hanoverian soldier pull the boot from his broken leg. He lived for some years after, but died in great poverty due to family fortunes having fallen low after a lawsuit

Fleming, Robert Mill of Achdregnie, Glenlivet

Forbes, ... Bellandy. Forced by the Highlanders to carry arms At home after Culloden.

Forbes, ... Bellandy   Killed
Forbes, Alexander Stabler, Peterhead   Servant to William Scott, late of Auchtydonald
Forbes, Alexander Tamore
Forbes, Alexander Labourer, Banff   Carlisle garrison
Forbes, Benjamin Merchant, Aberdeen   Was active from start to Culloden
Forbes, Benjamin, yr of Edinglassie Born after 1705, son of Lachlan Forbes of Edinglassie in Strathdon   Reported as having been wounded at Culloden, but managed to escape to France
Forbes, George Weaver, Fochabers, Morayshire
Forbes, George Aberdeen   At Culloden
Forbes, George, of Skellater Eldest son of George Forbes, 4th of Skellater and Isobel Gordon of Blelack   He married Christian Gordon, daughter of 'Old Glenbucket,' and had 3 sons, William, Ian Roy and Nathaniel   He survived Culloden and after some time in hiding, escaped to France   He never returned to live in Scotland, and died at Boulongne in Oct 1767, and his wife in January 1784 at Delhandy
Forbes, George An Aberdeenshire farmer living in Boghead in 1745   He was married and had two sons and one daughter
Forbes, James Labourer, Turnerhall, Ellon
Forbes, John Labourer, Kirk Culsalmond, Aberdeenshire
Forbes, John (see Lord Pitsligo)
Forbes, John Merchant   Candelmore, Banffshire
Forbes, John Strathbogie   Carlisle garrison
Forbes, John Wester-Achmore, Glenrinnes
Forbes, Jonathan, of Brux Farmer   Born in 1710, he was a Quaker and never married   He escaped capture at the battle of Culloden, and spent many years in hiding   Died 26 Oct 1801 in Aberdeen, aged 91
Forbes, Patrick Balivaler
Forbes, Robert Silversmith's apprentice in Aberdeen   Lurking after Culloden
Forbes, Robert Tenant of a farm 'within 11 miles of the town of Banff,' from which he supplied Cope's army with hay, corn and straw in September 1745   He was married to Anne Abernethie
Forbes, Robert Farmer, Corss, Aberdeen   Lieutenant, prisoner at Carlisle
Forbes, Robert Fifth son of John Forbes of Newe, baptised on 3 Nov 1727, he went with the Prince into England, but deserted on return to Stirling   He tried to get back to Carlisle where he had made friends, to work as a cabinetmaker, but was apprehended before he reached there by the Hanovarians   He was finally granted a free pardon and returned to Aberdeenshire and his parents
Forbes, The Rev Robert, MA Bishop of Ross and Caithness, he was born in 1708, son of Charles Forbes, schoolmaster of Rayne, Aberdeenshire and his wife, Marjory Wright   Took no part in the Rising since he was incarcerated the whole time, but the memorials he has left form one of the chief sources of the personal history of the Jacobites   He married (1) Agnes Gairey, in 1749 who died a few months later, and (2) Rachel Houston of Johnstone, Renfrew

Forbes, Thomas Vintner, Peterhead. Joined at Edinburgh.

Forbes, William Farmer, Wester Gauldwell, Boharm.

Forbes, William Banff. At Culloden, transported.

Forbes, William Born 1727, husbandman, Fochabers, Morayshire Transported 20 May 1747 from Tilbury

Forbes, William, in Edindiach Son of William Forbes, farmer in Edindiach, near Huntly, and his wife Mary Petrie, born in 1713   Married a daughter of Baillie John Cruickshank of Banff, and had one son, George Forbes, who became Sheriff-Substitute of Banff

Forrest, George Servant to the Countess of Erroll, Bowence, Cruden

Forrest, James Labourer, Nethermiln, Ellon   Joined after Preston

Forrest, William Ground officer to the Countess of Erroll, Gateside, Cruden Ground Officer at Gateside, Cruden

Forrest, William Labourer, Upper Braehead, Cruden   Joined after Preston

Forsyth, George Servant, Stoneywood, Newhills, Aberdeenshire   At Culloden

Forsyth, James Town Officer, Forres

Frain, John Farmer, Mill of Auchinhove, Lumphanan   Sergeant   Lurking after Culloden

Fraser, Alexander Servant at Castle Fraser, Clunie   At Falkirk and lurking after Culloden

Fraser, Alexander Gentleman, Miln of Artlock, Aberdeen   Volunteer

Fraser, Alexander Born 1725   Resident of Morayshire   Transported 20 Mar 1747 from London to Barbados in *Frere*.

Fraser, Charles, yr of Inverallochy Born in 1725, eldest son of Charles Fraser of Inverallochy and his wife, Anne, only daughter of John Udny of Udny   Killed at Culloden

Fraser, David Banffshire.   He was deaf and dumb but said to have killed 7 men   Transported 31 March 1747

Fraser, Donald Householder, Portsoy   Discharged

Fraser, James Strathbogie   Carlisle garrison

Fraser, James Auchriachan.

Fraser, James Upper Cults, Banffshire

Fraser, John Labourer, Aberdeen.

Fraser, John Balnacoull, Craigellachie

Fraser, Robert Carrier and Horsehirer, Banff

Fraser, Roderick Banffshire.

Fraser, Thomas Banff.   Prisoner at Stirling, shot in the thigh (surgeon's fee 6s 8d), escaped from hospital

Fraser, William, Inverallochy He was a brother of Charles Fraser, the owner of Inverallochy, living at Cairness.   He died in 1749 after being thrown by his horse.

Fullarton, John, yr of Dudwick Bowence, Cruden.   Eldest son of John Fullarton of Dudwick and his wife, Mary Falconer, daughter of Sir David Falconer of Newton.   After Culloden he wandered about the country disguised as a pedlar, and priced pigs.   He married Mary, daughter of Sir John Guthrie of King-Edward, but had no issue   She died at Aberdeen in 1805, aged 87; he died on 4 April 1768.

17

Gamatsgairn, Peter Born in Banff, taken at the River Esk   In Whitehaven Gaol

Garioch, Alexander Merchant in Aberdeen   Thought to have been the son of Alexander Garioch of Mergie, Kincardineshire   Surviving the Rising, he appears to have married Anne Bannnerman, daughter of Alexander Bannerman, and by her had four children   She died, aged 24, in 1772, near Aboyne, and Alexander at Aberdeen, 3 Feb 1802

Garmack, William Workman, Loanhead, Old Machar   At Culloden

Garry, Alexander Aberdeen   Carlisle garrison

Garvich, John Servant, Balquholly, Aberdeenshire   "A private man but very oppressive "

Garvoch, John Servant to Dorlaithers

Gatt, Alexander Servant to Arthur Gordon of Carnousie, Banff

Gattahon, John Turner, Dyce   Lurking after Culloden

Gauld, John Achnasgra, Braes of Glenlivet

Gauld, Robert Ruthven of Kirkmichael   "Insulted the country people "

Gauld, Thomas Achlanie, Tomintoul

Gauldie, James Pitchaish

Gaw, Lewis Knock of Achnail

Geddes, Alexander Labourer, Stanton, Huntly   Transported 5 May 1747 from Liverpool in *Gildart*, arrived Port North Potomac, Maryland 5 Aug 1747

Geddes, Andrew Aberdeenshire   Prisoner at Culloden   Died at Tilbury Fort

Gibb, Andrew Banff, Weaver   Drowned when going on board to be transported

Gibb, Andrew Tenant in Durn, Banffshire

Gibb, John Shoemaker, Aberdeen

Gibbon, William Servant to Menzies of Pitfoddels   Still a prisoner in London 9 Apr 1747

Gibenach, Donald Delavorar   Has submitted

Gibenach, Thomas Scalan, Banffshire

Gible, Henry Of Aberdeen   Prisoner in Carlisle

Gilbert, William Servant, Cushnie, Banffshire

Gill, Alexander Servant, Cushnie, Banff   Lurking after Culloden

Gill, Alexander Shipmaster in Fraserburgh   Eldest son of Alexander Gill, in the Mains of Pitfour, and Barbara Urquhart his wife, daughter of James Urquhart, Merchant in Fraserburgh   He married Isabel Catto, who was probably a daughter of George Catto in Fingask near Fraserburgh, and by her had three daughters

Gill, George Shoemaker, Bridgend, Aberdeenshire   At Inverurier battle

Gillespie, John Slater, Turriff   A Spy and "Reconnoitring" Officer

Glashan, George Servant, Bagrie Mill, Aberdeen

Glass, James Glenmuick   "An Officer, one of those who took the Excise officers prisoners for to deliver their books to him "

Glennie, William Gardener, Port of Aberdeen

Goodbrand, Alexander Born 1717, carpenter, Banff   30 years old, 5ft 6ins, brown hair and well made   Transported 5 May 1747 from Liverpool to

Leeward Islands in *Veteran*, but the ship was attacked off Antigua by a French privateer from Martinique. The Governor of Martinique refused English demands to hand the prisoners back, and granted the request of 10 to be sent to France possibly to negotiate for others

Goodbrand, John Wright, Cullen, Banff Lurking after Culloden.

Gordon, Alexander Resided at Refreish, Banffshire. A Lieutenant.

Gordon, Alexander Gentleman, Fochabers A Captain, "was at the affair of Keith, whereabouts not known "

Gordon, Alexander Backside of Clalshmore

Gordon, Alexander, of Craigwillie, near Huntly Must have been of mature age in the '45, and the Duchess of Gordon seems to have been interested in his liberation He and Robert Grant of Tamore had married sisters, the daughters of George Cumming of Reclettich (Mortlach) He survived the Rising

Gordon, Alexander, of Dorlaithers, sen Eldest son of George Gordon of Dorlaithers and Barbara Mackenzie of Ardloch. Survived Culloden, with his servant John Pirie, to whom he gave a liferent tack of Woodend, together with John Pirie, his son He died 2 June 1763, aged 58, and is buried with his wife, Helen, second daughter of Alexander Irvine of Drum, who died 6 December 1764, aged 64

Gordon, Alexander, jr of Dorlaithers Son of Alexander Gordon of Dorlaithers, Senior He succeeded his father and died, ummarried, 30 March 1768

Gordon, Rev Alexander Minister of Gairnside

Gordon, Rev Alexander Of Glencat family, a Roman Catholic priest Present at Culloden, and taken prisoner and lodged in the jail of Inverness where he died about three weeks later Son of John Gordon of Barrack and his wife, Joanna

Gordon, Alexander, of Letterfourie Farmer, Pattenbrungan, Banff Fourth son of James Gordon of Letterfourie and the daughter of Sir William Dunbar of Durn. Some time after the Rising he joined his brother James in Madeira He married, in 1778, Helen, daughter of Alexander Russell of Montcoffer, by whom he had three sons, James, Alexander and Charles Edward He died 16 Jan 1797, aged 82

Gordon, Alexander, of Binhall Elder brother of the better known Charles Eldest son of Patrick Gordon of Binhall, Cairnie, and his wife, a daughter of the Rev William Hay, Minister of Rothiemay Elected schoolmaster of Cairnie in 1742

Gordon, Arthur, of Carnousie Son of George Gordon of Carnousie, he was probably born about 1698. He married twice, (1) Mary, 3rd daughter of Alexander Duff of Drummuir, and widow of William Gordon of Lesmoir, and had one son, Alexander, (2) Isobel Campbell, widow of Robert Duff, his first wife's brother, by her his children were George, Arthur, Katherine, Jean and Anne. He escaped to France

Gordon, Charles Surgeon apprentice, Aberdeen.

Gordon, Charles Born 1730, son of Patrick Gordon. Resident of Binhall, Aberdeenshire Transported 1747 to Maryland

Gordon, Charles Strathaven   In Carlisle, transported, but drowned going on board ship

Gordon, Charles, of Binhall Third son of Patrick of Binhall, Cairnie, Baillie of Regality to the Duke of Gordon   Thought to be about 20, in 1745, but actually 17, and was a clerk to a writer in Edinburgh   Reprieved from hanging because of his youth, but remained in Newgate, and joined a mutiny there in 1747   In 1748 he returned to Scotland

Gordon, Charles, of Blelack Second son of Alexander of Blelack and Isobel Forbes "a masculine character "   In 1726 he succeeded his brother John   He married Anne Urquhart of Meldrum, whose mother was a Campbell of Cawdor   A Captain, he forced men out, and escaped imprisonment although he took part in the battles of Inverurie, Falkirk and Culloden, taking refuge in the manse of Towie, where he was fed by the minister's wife, Mrs Lumsden   He eventually returned peacefully to his ruined home, and died there in 1785, aged 80

Gordon, Charles, of Terpersie He and his son, James, were out in the '45, and their identities are confused in Lord Rosebery's List   He was over 60 and one of the first to be forced out by Glenbucket from his home in Aberdeenshire   He was tried and executed on 15 Nov 1746   He had been married for twenty years to Margaret, daughter of Adam Gordon at the Mill of Artloch, and there were nine children

Gordon, Charles, of Buckie Younger brother of George Gordon, laird of Buckie   Probably the same person who appears in Rosebery's List as "Charles Gordon, surgeon-apprentice, Aberdeen   Captain assisted in robbing Lord Sinclair of his horses near Portsoy on 7 May 1746   Whereabouts unknown "

Gordon, Charles, of Glastirem Brother of James Gordon of Glastirem

Gordon, Charles Gentleman, Eldornie, Banff

Gordon, David Second son of Old Glenbucket, he lived at Little Delavorar   He married in 1733, Isobel, daughter of Patrick Gordon of Kirkhill   Extremely active in the rebellion, assisting his father to force out unwilling recruits   He died, or was kill, in March 1746, a month before Cullodon leaving four daughters, his only son having died as an infant

Gordon, Donald Delavorar   Killed

Gordon, Duncan Aged 32, from Aberdeenshire   He was in Southward Gaol, described as 'not well'   Discharged 7 Mar 1747

Gordon, Francis Shoemaker, Aberdeen   Of the Tilphoudie family   Ensign   Lurking after Culloden

Gordon, Francis, of Kincardine Mill Son of George Gordon, heritor of Mill of Kincardine, Kincardine O'Neil, and Agnes Gordon   In 1731 he was apprenticed to Richard Gordon, Procurator-Fiscal of Aberdeenshire, and became an advocate   He was married to Barbara Rose, and had children, Hugh, Helen and Ann   On retreat from Derby, with Arthur Gordon of Carnousie, made an offer to Cumberland to secure a pardon   This was not accepted   He escaped to France after 1746, and entered the French service, where he was shortly afterwards killed in action

20

Gordon, George Tomintoul. Killed.

Gordon, George Blacksmith, Cullen

Gordon, George Newtown of Glenlivet.

Gordon, George Farmer, Muiryfold, Grange.

Gordon, George, of Glenbucket Third son of the famous Major-General John Gordon, 'Old Glenbucket' He survived Cullodon, and escaped from prison in Inverness. He became a doctor in Jamaica, where he died.

Gordon, George, of Birkenbush He was married to Katherine, daughter of Charles Gordon of Glengerack He died in 1752 Known to have played an active part in Banffshire

Gordon, George, of Buckie He married, on 21 Oct 1746, Anna Gordon of Cairnfield, and had a son, Captain John, who was the last laird of Buckie Died March 1756.

Gordon, George, of Hallhead Eldest son of Robert Gordon of Hallhead and Esslemont and his wife, Isabel Byres. Robert Gordon was a merchant in Bordeaux. Married in January 1729, Amy Bowdler, an Englishwoman, daughter of Thomas Bowdler, and had one child, Robert, born 1732. He was at Boulogne between 1749 and 1750, and in 1756 lived in Bordeaux

Gordon, George Brother of John Gordon of Beldorney Second son of Gordon of Beldorney and his wife Mary, daughter of John Gordon of Law and Wardhouse. He was in prison in Aberdeen on 14 Dec 1746

Gordon, George Eldest son of Thomas Gordon, Fodderletter He died in 1764 at Leith, as Manager of the Cudbear Works.

Gordon, George Priest Born in Fochabers, and ordained priest in Sept 1725

Gordon, Henrietta, Dowager Duches of Born a Mordaunt, daughter of the Earl of Peterborough, she married the second Duke of Gordon, who died in 1728 On agreeing to bring up her large family of four sons and seven daughters in the Protestant faith, from 1735 to 1745 received a Government pension of £1,000 a year She died in 1760

Gordon, Ishmael Servant, Gaulrig, Banffshire.

Gordon, James Achlanie. An Officer Killed

Gordon, James Banffshire. Prisoner at Inverness.

Gordon, James Born 1719. Resident of Birkenbush, Cullen, Banffshire Transported 1747 from London

Gordon, James, yr of Aberlour Son of Patrick Gordon of Aberlour, and married to Clementina Gordon, daughter of George Gordon of Buckie.

Gordon, James Croft of Minmore.

Gordon, James, of Cobairdy Son of Sir James Gordon, 2nd Baronet of Park, by his second wife Margaret Elphinstone, widow of George Leslie of Balquhain. Probably born in 1723. He married Mary Forbes, daughter of James, 15th Lord Forbes, who is described as "a very sweet tempered woman, but not very handsome," and by her had James, born 1742, Ernest, born 1743, and William, born 1744 He escaped to France, and in 1747 was living at Cleves He died in Aberdeen on 11 May 1773.

21

Gordon, James, of Glastirem   Son of George Gordon of Glastirem, belonging to a Roman Catholic family.   He married, in 1738, Mary, daughter of Charles Hay of Rannes, who was also widow of John Leith of Leith Hall   He surrendered at Fochabers   He seems to have been a man of weak character, much under the influence of others   He married again once more, and died on 22 Feb 1783, aged 64

Gordon, James Younger brother of Birkenbush   Very active, wounded at Inverurie skirmish   He seems to have recovered, as he married Elizabeth Gordon and had issue

Gordon, James, sen of Terpersie, Banff

Gordon, James, yr of Terpersie Born 1732, son of James Gordon David Gordon of Kirkhill, Glenbucket's son, captured young Terpersie while out fishing, and carried him off to join the army when only 15 or 16 He was involved in the riot in Southwark Gaol in December 1747, and was finally discharged 1 Aug 1748   He emigrated to Jamaica in 1748 becoming a mahogany cutter there

Gordon, John Younger brother of George Gordon, Fodderletter   Deceased by 1746

Gordon, John Schoolmaster, Tarrycroys, Keith   Eldest son of Patrick Gordon of Binhall

Gordon, John Farmer, Borter, Banff   Acted as spy and was taken prisoner

Gordon, John Tynavoir, Tomintoul   Prisoner

Gordon, John Born 1728, weaver, resident in Loynavere, Elgin, Morayshire Transported 5 May 1747 from Liverpool to Leeward Islands in *Veteran*, but the ship was attacked off Antigua by a French privateer from Martinique   The Governor of Martinique refused English demands to hand the prisoners back, and granted the request of 10 to be sent to France possibly to negotiate for others

Gordon, John Clashmore, Ensign   His house was burnt

Gordon, John Inchnacape, Tomintoul

Gordon, John Servant to Carnousie

Gordon, John, of Avochie Son of Harry Gordon of Avochie   He cannot have been more than a lad at the time of the Rising   He must have escaped to France, and seems probably that he remained there until 1763   He married Mary, only child of Peter Gordon of Ardmeallie, a noted Whig   They had three sons and two daughters   He died at Aberdeen in April 1778

Gordon, John, of Beldorney Born 22 April 1723, son of J Gordon of Beldorney and Mary, daughter of John Gordon of Law and Wardhouse   Married on 4 Sept 1745, Margaret Frances, daughter of Patrick Smyth of Methven   Died Oct 1760, and his wife died in Dundee on 23 Dec 1791   They had several children, among them Alexander and Charles Edward

Gordon, John Younger brother of George Gordon, Fodderletter   Deceased by 1746

Gordon, John Chamberlain to Duke of Gordon   Prisoner Inverness in April 1746

22

Gordon, John, of Glenbucket The famous "Old Glenbucket" of the '15 and '45. He was born about 1673 and was about 74 years old in 1747 Son of John Gordon of Glenbucket, he married in 1702, Jean, elder daughter of Harry Forbes of Boyndlie, and had four sons, John, David, George and Alexander, and six daughters, Helen, Isobel, Christian, Henrietta, Clementina, and Cecilia. Fled via Norway to Sweden after Culloden, and settled in Boulogne sur Mer, France

Gordon, John Eldest son of "Old Glenbucket", he seems to have been somewhat degenerate Born in 1707, he married about 1728 Ann, daughter of Sir Alexander Lindsay of Evelack, and had a son, William

Gordon, John Farmer of Colonach, Huntly May have been the son of Alexander Gordon of Colonach, son of Alexander of Beldorney

Gordon, John, of Cordregny

Gordon, John, of Minmore Was eldest son of William Gordon, third laird of Minmore He married and had four sons, William, who succeeded him in Minmore, Lewis, John and Henry He died in August 1776.

Gordon, John Priest at Preshome Son of Peter Gordon, wadsetter, Birkenbush, was born in 1706 He died 9 Nov 1752, aged 46

Gordon, Lewis Miln of Laggan. Carried arms and collected cess

Gordon, Lord Lewis Born 1724, 3rd son of Alexander, 2nd Duke of Gordon, who died in 1728, and his wife, Lady Henrietta, daughter of Charles, Earl of Peterborough He acted as Governor of Aberdeen Escaped to France where he was described in a MS in the French Foreign Office as "very reckless and obstinate, and sometimes so much deranged as to have to be shut up." Died Montreuil on 15 Jun 1754

Gordon, Ludovick Merchant, Elgin Lurking after Culloden

Gordon, Patrick, of Cordregny

Gordon, Peter Innkeeper, Strathbogie

Gordon, Robert Prisoner at Carlisle

Gordon, Robert Nether Clashmore

Gordon, Rev Robert Roman Catholic Priest, younger brother of Patrick Gordon of Kirkhill Born in 1687 He was charged with being a spy, and jailed in Newgate On his release he went to Holland, and then to Paris and Rome. He died at Lens, France in 1764, aged 77

Gordon, Robert, jun of Logie Son of Alexander Gordon, 3d of Logie. He succeeded his father in 1752, and sold Logie. He married and had two sons, Alexander and James.

Gordon, Robert, of Craigwillie Son of Alexander Gordon of Craigwillie

Gordon, Thomas Farmer, Strathbogie Born 1689 Transported from London to Jamaica or Barbados on 31 March 1747

Gordon, Thomas, Fodderletter Son of George Gordon of Fodderletter He married Isabella, daughter of John Macpherson of Invereshie He had four sons, George, John, James and William.

Gordon, William Farmer, Newmill, Banff. Lurking after Culloden.

Gordon, William Farmer, Ferrar, Aboyne. Lurking after Culloden

Gordon, William Dell, Avonside.

Gordon, William Glenrinnes.

Gordon, William Aberdeen. Prisoner in Inverness.

Gordon, William Grandson of Glenbucket Son of John Gordon, younger, of Glenbucket, and his wife, Ann Lindsay He was only 15 or 16 at the time of the Rising He had a son, who in turn had a son, Charles, the last male descendant of Gordon of Glenbucket

Gordon, William Merchant and Ground Officer to the Duke of Gordon Was a prisoner in Tilbury, and possibly the same person described in Lord Rosebery's List as "William Gordon, Glenrinnes"

Gordon, Sir William of Park Eldest son of Sir James Gordon of Park and his wife, Helen Fraser, born in 1712 He married in June 1745, Janet Duff, second daughter of Lord Braco It is said she eloped with him from Rothiemay, leaping from a window She was 15 years younger than he, being only 18 He escaped abroad after Culloden and his wife followed him to France He had a daughter, and a son, John James, born 26 March 1749 and William, born 1750 He died of a fever in Douai on 5 June 1751 His widow returned to Scotland and married George Hay of Mountblairy She died in 1758

Gow, Alexander Ruthven in Kirkmichael

Gow, William Salmon fisher, Don Bridge, Old Machar At Culloden

Grant, Alexander Nether Cluny Carried arms in the character of an officer

Grant, Alexander Carpenter, Aberdeen Transported 31 Mar 1747 from London, 5 May 1747 from Liverpool to Leeward Islands in *Veteran*, but the ship was attacked off Antigua by the French, who released all prisoners in Martinique June 1747

Grant, Alexander Brother to Neivie

Grant, Alexander Calier, Glenlivet

Grant, Alexander Backside of Clashmore

Grant, Alexander Deskie, Glenrinnes

Grant, Alexander Farmer, Croftbain

Grant, Alexander, of Netherclunie, Banffshire A prisoner in the New Gaol, Southward in Oct 1746, and acquitted 15 December

Grant, Alexander Logan of Blairfindy

Grant, Charles Tomdonach, Glenlivet Lieutenant and deserted

Grant, David Old Meldrum

Grant, David Son of Blairfindy, "An officer" who returned to Blairfindy with his father

Grant, Donald Easter Gaulrig, Tomintoul

Grant, Elizabeth Born 1727, seamstress, Banff Transported 20 Mar 1747

Grant, Grigor Delavorar

Grant, Humphrey Weaver, Banff A Lieutenant in the Duke of Perth's Regiment

Grant, James Miller in Inchnacape His house was burnt

Grant, James Fiddler, Haddo, Banffshire

Grant, James Delnabo, Tomintoul

Grant, James, Logan of Blairfindy Said to have gone to Canada

Grant, John Servant, Haddo, Banffshire

Grant, John Servant to Sir W Gordon of Park Lurking after Culloden.

Grant, John Loanbeg, Banffshire

Grant, John Croftbain

Grant, John Farmer, Glenlivet.
Grant, John, jun Deskie, Banffshire.
Grant, John Inverlochy, Glenconglass   His house was burnt
Grant, John Merchant, Tomintoul
Grant, John Son of John Grant, Merchant, Tomintoul
Grant, John Upper Drumin
Grant, John Weaver, Tombreck
Grant, John Tailor, Strathbogie, Aberdeen   Lurking after Culloden
Grant, John Born 1713, weaver, Banff   Transported 5 May 1747 from Liverpool to Virginia in *Johnson*, arrived Port Oxford, Maryland 5 Aug 1747
Grant, John Tomnavoulin, Glenlivet
Grant, John Son of Blairfindy   "A Lieutenant in the Jacobite Army but deserted "
Grant, John Roy Demickmore, Glenlivet
Grant, John Roy Wheelwright, Aberdeen   In the Tolbooth
Grant, Lewis Little Nevie.   Was at the spoiling of Cullen House
Grant, Neil Tomaclagan, Glenconglass.
Grant, Patrick Inchnacape.
Grant, Peter Delavorar
Grant, Peter Wester Fodderletter
Grant, Peter Gaulrig   Was forced out, and twice deserted
Grant, Peter The last survivor of those who fought at Culloden   He was born in 1714 at Dubrach, a small farm in Braemar and was a tailor to trade   In 1821 he received an allowance of a guinea a week from George IV, and died 11 Feb 1824   His tombstone eads "To the memory of Peter Grant, sometime farmer in Dunbrach, were he was born in 1714, died at Auchindryne, aged 110 "   His wife, Mary Cumming died in 1811   She was 32 years his junior   He had a daughter, Annie, who died in 1860
Grant, Peter Roy Badiglashean, Ballindalloch
Grant, Robert Aberdeenshire   Prisoner at Culloden
Grant, William Banffshire   Prisoner at Culloden
Grant, William Born 1699, linen weaver, Aberdeen   Transported 5 May 1747 from Liverpool to Virginia in *Gildart*, arriving Port North Potomac, Maryland, 5 Aug 1747.
Grant, William Tomintoul.
Grant, William, Mr A Popish Priest, Balivalier, Banffshire
Grant, William Clagan, Glenlivet
Grant, William Tomnavoulin, Glenlivet
Grant, William Gaulrig.
Grant, William Findran, Banffshire
Grant, William, of Blairfindy In June 1746, described as being "at home," although his house was burnt by Cumberland's troops
Grant, William Fodderletter.
Grant, William Roy Balnacoull, Craigellachie.
Gray, John Servant, Keith.

Grant, John Servant, Keith, Banffshire   In Carlisle garrison   Transported 5 May 1747 from Liverpool to Virginia in *Gildart*, arriving Port North Potomac, Maryland, 5 Aug 1747

Gray, William Salmon fisher, Don Bridge   At Culloden, taken prisoner but admitted to bail

Gray, William Salmon fisher, Fochabers   Was at plundering of Cullen House

Guissoch, John Avochie's Regiment, of Aberdeen   Prisoner at Culloden

Gunn, John Servant to James Moir at Stoneywood   He must have been middle-aged in 1745 because he was "out" in 1715   Described as a person of immense size, who married a gipsy

Guthrie, James Servant, Rannes   Very active   Lurking after Culloden

Hacket, Alexander Farmer at Drachlaw Mill   He was probably employed on his father's farm (Charles Hacket, sen)

Hacket (or Halket), Charles Born 1727   Labourer, Aberdeen   5ft 9 5ins, well made, sprightly   Probably son of Charles Hacket, sen, Drachlaw Mill, Aberdeenshire   Transported 5 May 1747 from Liverpool to Leeward Islands in *Veteran*, but the ship was attacked off Antigua by a French privateer from Martinique   The Governor of Martinique refused English demands to hand the prisoners back, and granted the request of 10 to be sent to France possibly to negotiate for others

Hacket, Charles, sen "A violent Jacobite "   He farmed at Drachlaw Mill, Aberdeenshire, on the banks of the Deveron   He had at least three sons, Charles, Alexander and James

Hacket, Charles, jun Described as "Writer's servant "   Son of Charles Hacket, farmer, Drachlaw Mill, Banffshire   He survived the Rising and married Helen Smith, daughter and heiress of Patrick Smith of Inveramsey and settled down as life renter of the property, living in the house of Poolwall where he became a zealous and successful agriculturist   He died in 1809 aged 85

Hacket, James Described as "a farmer's son, Drachlamiln "   He was probably the eldest son of Charles Hacket, farmer, Drachlaw Mill, Deveronside   He was in hiding after Culloden and possibly went to France

Hall, Alexander Salmon fisher, Kincoussie, Maryculter   Sergeant   Lurking after Culloden.

Hamilton, Elizabeth Born 1725, seamstress, Banff   22 years old, 5ft, brown hair and thin   Taken at Carlisle with her husband Edward Clavering from Northumberland, who was executed at York in 1746   Transported 5 May 1747 from Liverpool to Leeward Islands in *Veteran*, but the ship was attacked off Antigua by a French privateer from Martinique   The Governor of Martinique refused English demands to hand the prisoners back, and granted the request of 10 to be sent to France possibly to negotiate for others

Hamilton, John, of Sandstown or Sandiestown, near Huntly (Huntly Lodge) Factor to the Duke of Gordon on the Strathbogie part of the estate   Was Governor of Carlisle Castle at the time of its surrender   He was executed at Kennington Common on 28 November 1746, and his head was set up on the Gates of Carlisle.   His widow was Janet Mitchell.   He was over 60 years in 1745.

Hasben, James Banff.   Ogilvie's Regiment.   Prisoner at Culloden

Hay, Adam, of Asleid He was the son of Andrew Hay, a merchant, who died in his infancy and his wife, Christian Cummine, Lady Asleid   Taken prison at Culloden.   He said he was taken from his mother's house in Aberdeenshire in Sept 1745 by seven Highlanders, escaped in the night, and was taken again   On 28 July 1748 he received a pardon upon condition of banishment for life

Hay, Adam, of Cairnbanno, New Deer

Hay, Alexander Blacksmith, Fochabers, Moray   Lurking after Culloden

Hay, Alexander Gentleman, Aswanley, Banff   He was sentenced to death on 20 December 1746

Hay, Andrew, yr of Rannes   Born in 1713, he was the eldest son of Charles Hay of Rannes, who married Helen, only child of Dr Andrew Fraser of Inverness.   He was 7ft 2ins tall   He went into hiding after Culloden, and went abroad in 1752.   In 1762, when most exiles had returned home, he remained reluctant to do so because of his size, but did so in 1763, and his mother, over 80 years, was there to receive him   He died, unmarried, 29 Aug 1789, aged 76

Hay, George, of Mountblairy Second son of Andrew Hay of Mountblairy, WS   He was probably under 20 years at the time of the Rising, and was said to look 15   He married in 1753 Janet Duff, widow of Sir William Gordon of Park, who was then 25 years old, and after her death in 1758 he married Miss Peggy Sinclair of Scotscalder, leaving issue   He was a prisoner in London, having been taken before Culloden   He died peacefully in Edinburgh on 2 July 1771

Hay, George Sailor, Portsoy.   He was carried to London on *HMS Winchester*, but escaped on landing, and went to France

Hay, James Ensign in Lord Pitsligo's Regiment

Hay, John Wright, Delgaty, Aberdeenshire   A recruiting officer and the principal person who "proclaimed the Pretender at Turriff and drank rebellious healths."

Hay, Mary, Countess of Erroll Eldest daughter of John, 12th Earl of Erroll and his wife, Lady Anne Drummond, only daughter of James, 3rd Earl of Perth   She became Countess of Erroll on the death of her unmarried brother, Charles, in 1717.   Before Aug 1722 she married Alexander Falconer of Newton, and he assumed the surname of Hay of Delgaty and died in July 1745   There were no children of the marriage   She was a strong Jacobite supporter   She died aged 78 on 19 Aug 1758

Hector, John Born 30 Aug 1705, son of James Hector and Margart Clerk. Salmon fisher, Cruives, Old Machar, Aberdeen   Transported 5 May 1747 from Liverpool to Virginia in *Johnson*, arrived Port Oxford, Maryland 5 Aug 1747.

Hepburn, Peter Farmer, Ardin, Aberdeenshire.   Had a commission from Gordon of Glenbucket to recruit.

Hendry, John Parish of Skene   Deserted from Guise's Regiment

Hendry, Robert Durn, Banff   Servant to Sir William Dunbar

Hendry, Sanders   Private in Duke of Perth's Regiment, of Wardmill, Aberdeen   At Carlisle

Henry, or Hendry, William Aged 14, of Wardmill in Aberdeenshire went along with his father, Sanders Henry, a private man in the Duke of Perth's Regiment, who left him at Carlisle   After imprisonment in the Cathedral he was moved to Chester Gaol, where there were a number of other young boys, aged from 7 to 14, and some girls, who seem to have accompanied their parents from the North of Scotland   Eventually some were pardoned and transported, and the women and children were discharged 13 Feb 1747

Hogg, John Extraordinary Tidesman, Aberdeen

Hosie, ... Servant to Brux   Farmer in Dukerton

Hunter, John Labourer, Lochshangie, Kemnay   Lurking after Culloden.

Hutcheson, Thomas Merchant, Elgin   Lurking after Culloden

Imbry, Alexander Lochloun, Banchory   Lurking after Culloden.

Ingram, John Workman, Loanhead, Old Machar   At Culloden

Ingram, John Miller, Perrys Miln, Aberdeenshire

Innes, Alexander Balmdrarvan   Forced out and deserted

Innes, Alexander, of Cowie and Breda, Commissary of Aberdeen Second son of John Innes, 7th of Edingight, and Jean, daughter of Patrick Duff of Craigston, born 12 July 1727   Admitted a member of the Society of Advocates in Aberdeen 29 Jan 1752   He married in 1767, Elizabeth, daughter of William Davidson of Midmar Castle (d at Cowie 8 July 1795, aged 48)   He died in June 1788   They had two sons and eight daughters, among them John, William, and Jane

Innes, Alexander, of Clerkseat Second son of Alexander Innes of Inaltrie and his wife, Isobel Anderson, born in 1710   He married Anna Rose, by whom he had 7 sons and 11 daughters   He died 12 March 1789

Innes, Colonel James Cullen, Banffshire   Third son of Sir Alexander Innes 1st Baronet of Coxton, Morayshire   Overseer of the county roads of Banffshire   He had been in the 1715 Rising, and was nearly 70 years of age in 1746   On 21 Oct 1746 he was executed with seven others at Brampton, nine miles from Carlisle   He left a wife, Mary Ramsay (d 24 Sept 1747) and a family of daughters

Innes, Sir James Second son of Sir George Innes, 2nd Baronet of Coxton, and his wife Elizabeth, daughter and heiress of John Gordon of Rothiemay, born in 1715   He inherited no property, and is described as a weaver of Techmurie, Tyrie, Aberdeen   Later he became tenant of Achanacy, near Keith   He married Margaret, daughter of James Brodie of Muiresk (d 1786), and had 3 sons and 4 daughters, among them James Sir John, Sir David and Elizabeth   He died 3 June 1790

Innes, James of Balnacraig Second, but eldest surviving son of Charles Innes, wadsetter of Drumnagesk, and Claudia Irvine, only daughter and heiress of Captain Robert Irvine   Married Catherine Gordon, niece of Bishop Geddes (d 5 May 1790, aged 85) and had 3 sons and 2 daughters   Lurking after Culloden. He died 11 Feb 1780

Innes, James Wigmaker, Fochabers, Moray   Free after Culloden

Innes, John Of Buchan Prisoner in Inverness.

Innes, John Wright, Aberdeen Acted as Ensign Lurking after Culloden.

Innes, John Balmdrarvan. Forced out.

Innes, John Wright, Aberdeen

Innes, John Younger son of Alexander Innes of Inaltrie and his wife, Isobel Anderson, born in 1719 Described as a dyster in Turriff He died without issue before 1768

Innes, John, yr of Edingight Eldest son of John Innes, 7th of Edingight, who married Jean Duff, eldest daughter and one of the 36 children of Patrick Duff of Craigston Born 21 Feb 1721, he married in August 1753, Elizabeth, daughter of Captain Lewis Grant of Carron, and had 4 sons and 5 daughters He died at "Castle Panton" on 7 June 1790 whilst Provost of Banff, and his wife died on 22 March 1803

Innes, Patrick Weaver, Edindiach, Banffshire Lurking after Culloden

Innes, Robert Born 1721, resident of Banff Fiddler to Charles Gordon of Buckie. Transported 31 March 1747 from London to Jamaica in *St George* or *Carteret*, arriving Jamaica 1747

Innes, William Wigmaker, Fochabers Transported 31 March 1747 from London to Barbados in *Frere*

Innes, William Born 1721, fiddler, Buckie, Banffshire Transported 31 Mar 1747 from London to Jamaica in *St George* or *Carteret*, arriving Jamaica 1747

Irons, Robert Aberdeenshire Released in London

Irvine, Adam Bruchly, Down, Banff Son of Rev Robert Irvine, minister of Towie, and his second wife, Agnes, daughter of Patrick Murray of Blairfindy. In 1710 he married Margaret, daughter of Sir John Reid of Barra, against her parents wishes They arranged to be married in the wood nearby her home, by an old minister named Donald Mackintosh When, a few days later this was discovered, the bride's father turned her out, and she joined her husband They had two sons, Robert and Kenneth, and 2 daughters, Margaret and Barbara Lurking after Culloden

Irvine, Alexander, of Drum Son of Alexander Irvine of Drum and Isabel Thonmson, his wife, daughter of Thomas Thomson of Faichfield He married in 1751, Mary, second daughter of James Ogilvie of Auchiries (d 5 April 1796) and by her had 3 sons and 3 daughters, Alexander, Charles, James, Margaret, Isabel and Rebecca Lurking after Culloden. He died 9 Feb 1761

Irvine, Charles Surgeon, Aberdeen

Irvine, James Servant to William Booth, Aberdeen "Under suspicion for having been out of town when the army was here "

Jack, Andrew Born 1717, husbandman, Elgin, Morayshire Transported 1747 from Tilbury

Jack, William Born 1711, merchant and messenger, Elgin, Morayshire Transported 31 Mar 1747 from Tilbury to Barbados

Jaffrey, George Servant to William Booth, Aberdeen

Jaffrey, James Joiner, Aberdeen At Falkirk, and lurking after Culloden.

Jaffrey, Thomas Under Gaoler, Aberdeen Lurking after Culloden.

Johnston, James "Bleetcher," Aberdeen
Johnston, John Servant, Burnhead or Burnend, Carnousie, Aberdeenshire Lurking after Culloden
Johnston, John Born 11 Sept 1739, son of William Johnston, Marnoch, Banffshire Resident in Banff Transported 1747 from Tilbury
Johnston, Robert Born 1701, labourer, Stonehaven, Kincardineshire Transported 31 March 1747 for Jamaica or Barbados
Johnstone, William Aberdeen Turned evidence at the York trials and was released
Joiner, David Born 1727, labourer, Aberdeen Aged 20, brown hair, 5ft 2ins Transported 5 May 1747 from Liverpool to Leeward Islands in *Veteran*, but the ship was attacked off Antigua by a French privateer from Martinique The Governor of Martinique refused English demands to hand the prisoners back, and granted the request of 10 to be sent to France possibly to negotiate for others
Jopp (or Japp), John Born 1731 Carpenter, Banff Carlisle garrison Transported 5 May 1747 from Liverpool to Leeward Islands in *Veteran*, but the ship was attacked off Antigua by a French privateer from Martinique The Governor of Martinique refused English demands to hand the prisoners back, and granted the request of 10 to be sent to France possibly to negotiate for others
Joyner, James Householder, Portsoy, Banffshire
Joyner, James Servant, Towks, Banff Lurking after Culloden
Joyner, James Aberdeen Taken at Carlisle
Keith, David Workman, Hardgate, Old Machar Lurking after Culloden.
Keith, George Born 12 Sept 1714, Old Machar, Aberdeen, shoemaker Well made, 5ft 11 5ins, black hair Parents George Keith and Isobel Leys, transported 5 May 1747 from Liverpool to Leeward Islands in *Veteran*, but the ship was attacked off Antigua by a French privateer from Martinique The Governor of Martinique refused English demands to hand the prisoners back, and granted the request of 10 to be sent to France possibly to negotiate for others
Keith, James Born 1727, servant, Glenvervie, Kincardineshire Transported 24 Feb 1747 from Liverpool to Virginia in *Gildart*, arriving Port North Potomac, Maryland 5 Aug 1747
Kemlo (or Kemno), Joseph Blacksmith, Hardgate, Old Machar, Aberdeen Transported 24 Feb 1747 from Liverpool to Virginia in *Gildart*, arriving Port North Potomac, Maryland 5 Aug 1747
Kennedy, John Deskie
Kennedy, Robert Durn
Kerr, Alexander Weaver, Keith, Banffshire Private man, hired out Lurking after Culloden
Kilgour, Peter Dyster, Ellon
King, James Born 1726, labourer or servant, Darrow, Banff Transported 22 Apr 1747 from Liverpool to Virginia in *Johnson*, arriving Port Oxford Maryland, 5 Aug 1747
Kinloch, Alexander Fochabers, Morayshire, merchant Son of Sir John Kinloch of Kinloch and Elizabeth Nevay Transported 14 Aug 1748

Kisaach, John Born 16 Feb 1724, Alves, Morayshire, son of John Kisaach and Margaret Smith. Shoemaker in Alves Transported 19 Mar 1747 from Tilbury

Knows, Robert Salmon fisher, Craighead, Nether Banchory Prisoner in Aberdeen

Knows (or Knowles), William Born 16 July 1713, son of John Knowles and Barbara Malcolm Salmon fisher, Nether Banchory, Kincardineshire Transported 24 Feb 1747 from Liverpool to Virginia in *Gildart*, arriving Port North Potomac, Maryland 5 Aug 1747

Kynnach, John Burnt-brae, Alvah

Laing, John Labourer, Turnhall, Ellon.

Laing, Thomas Leadmine worker, Livingstones Yards, Aberdeen Transported 24 Feb 1747 from Liverpool to Virginia in *Gildart*, arriving Port North Potomac, Maryland, 5 Aug 1747

Laing, William Servant, Fochabers, Moray

Lamb, William Achnakyle, Banffshire

Lamond, John (or Joseph) Born 1721 Resident of Aberdeen Groom to the Duke of Perth Transported 24 Feb 1747 from Liverpool to Virginia in *Gildart*, arriving Port North Potomac, Maryland, 5 Aug 1747

Largs (or Largo), Joseph Journeyman Saddler, Aberdeen At Culloden

Laurie, James Shoemaker, Banff Prisoner, but discharged

Law, George He was born in Crimond, Buchan, and in 1745 was 40 years of age and living in Aberdeen Nonjurant Minister, and Chaplain to Stoneywood's regiment, captured on the night of Culloden Had a son, William Despite strong evidence of involvement, he was acquitted at his trial in London

Law, William Son of Rev George Law A schoolboy in 1745, he accompanied his father No proceedings were taken against him

Lawrance, John Wright's apprentice, Aberdeen Discharged 15 July 1747

Lawrance, William Farmer, Lochlip, Rathen Eldest son of William Lawrance (1692-1751), farmer, at Craigellie, Lonmay He was born about 1714 He married about 1742, Margaret Mitchell, and had issue. Died after 19 July 1761.

Lawrence, John Mason, Keith, Moray Lurking after Culloden Presumed grandfather of Alexander Lawrence, surgeon, RN d 23 May 1835 aged 43

Lawrence, John Merchant, Old Deer Eldest son of Robert Lawrence in Auchmachar and his wife Elspet May Born at Skillimarno, Old Deer, 25 June 1701.

Lawson, Alexander In Badentoy Apprehended for harbouring rebels Prisoner in Aberdeen

Ledderkin, Alexander Aberdeen Monaltrie's Regiment, prisoner at Culloden

Legat, George Merchant and tailor, Ellon, "always kept rejoicing when the rebels met with success."

Leigh, Alexander Wigmaker, Elgin Prompted others to join the Rising At home after Culloden

31

Leith, Alexander Mason, Hillhead of Turriff, Aberdeenshire Lurking after Culloden

Leith, Alexander Farmer, Collithie, Parish of Gartly, Aberdeenshire He was at least 50 years when he went into England with the Jacobites Prisoner at Carlisle He was executed 28 Nov 1746 On the eve of his execution he wrote to his brother that the child of Elizabeth Anderson who, on his advice had named John Chisholm as the father was in fact his

Leith, John Innkeeper, Strathbogie, Aberdeenshire Lurking after Culloden

Leith, Mrs Anne Sometimes described as the Florence Nightingale of the Rising She had a young son called Alexander, whom she put to school in Inverness at the time of the Rising She, with her maid, Eppy tended to the wounded on the field of Culloden, and thereafter helped the prisoners in Inverness with ministrations and messages She was married to a cousin of Gordon of Glenbucket, and had three young sons

Leith, Anthony Farmer. Bogs of Leith Hall, Kennethmont He was 5th and youngest son of John Leith of Leith Hall, Kennethmont, and his wife Janet Ogilvie daughter of George, second Lord Banff He was eventually captured after Culloden, tried and transported He married Jean Hay

Leith, George Third son of John Leith of Leith Hall At some time after the Rising he lived at Blackhall

Leith, George Salmon fisher and tidesman, Aberdeen

Leith, John Innkeeper, Strathbogie. Aberdeenshire Lurking after Culloden

Leith, Lawrence Described as Farmer, New Flinder, Kinethmond Fourth son of John Leith of Leith Hall He was a prisoner at Aberdeen on 11 Aug 1746 and was transported He returned, and died in Aberdeen in his 65th year on 18 Jan 1778

Leith, Patrick Second son of John Leith of Leith Hall

Leith, The Rev Robert Catholic priest, and brother of Alexander Leith Arrested on suspicion of complicity on board the *St Quentin* 16 Nov 1747

Leith, William Resident in Aberdeen, prisoner there

Leith, William Tobacconist, Old Aberdeen At Culloden, prisoner in Elgin

Leslie, Alexander Farmer, Auchinhanich, Banffshire Ensign Lurking after Culloden

Leslie, James Labouring servant, Old Meldrum

Leslie, John Labourer, Old Meldrum

Leslie, John, 7th Laird of Warthill

Leslie, William A farmer's son, Hillhead of Turriff Lurking after Culloden

Lew, James Banffshire Prisoner at Southwark

Ley, Thomas Labourer, Tullich, Glenmuick Lurking after Culloden.

Ley, William Deserter from the army, Charlestown, Aboyne A Sergeant Lurking after Culloden.

Lind, George Labouring servant, Old Meldrum

Lind, George Smith, Old Meldrum

Lines, Andrew Labourer, Blackhall, Strachan, Aberdeenshire   A Sergeant
Lurking after Culloden.

Logie, Patrick Writer, Aberdeen   Acted as Land Waiter and Officer of
Excise   Lurking after Culloden.

Logie, William Porter, Elgin   "Very active in giving intelligence to Rebels "
Lurking after Culloden

Longmuir, Charles Labourer, Upper Torrie, Nigg,   Lurking after Culloden.

Lorimer, William Farmer, Ironhill, Pitsligo

Low, John Farmer, Gowry Hall, Aboyne   A Sergeant

Lowpen (or Lowper), Alexander   Mason, Strathbogie, Aberdeenshire
Lurking after Culloden

Luckie, John Born 20 Oct 1728, St Nicholas, Aberdeen, son to William
Luckie and Helen Black   Shoemaker, Aberdeen   Prisoner
Transported 24 Feb 1747 from Liverpool to Virginia in *Gildart*, arriving
Port North Potomac, Maryland, 5 Aug 1747

Lumsden, David Farmer in Mains of Auchlossan, Lumphanan   Killed at
Culloden   Son of John Lumsden in Cromar and his wife, whose name
was Irvine, he had children named James, Harry, John and Margaret

Lumsden, John Farmer, Mill of Coull   Youngest son of John Lumsden in
Cromar, and brother of David in Mains of Acuhlossan   Although he
only bought and furnished shoes for the Jacobites, he was obliged to
go into hiding after the Rising.   He married Katherine, daughter of
Robert Reid of Balbrydie, by whom he had two sons

Lumsden, John, of Ardhuncart, Kildrummy Killed at Culloden   Son of
John Lumsden, "The Old Turk", who died before 1740 and his mother
was Helen Shireff, who died in 1744, aged 72

McAdam, William Shenval   Deserted September 1745

McAlister, Alexander Tomnavoulin, Glenlivet

McAllan, John Tomintoul

McAlpin, Patrick Gaulrig

McAndrew, John Servant to John MacAndrew in Glenmuick

MacAndrew, John Monaltrie's Regiment, Aberdeen   Prisoner at Culloden

McAngus, William Lettoch, Glenrinnes

McConnach, John Servant to Charles Gordon of Blelack

McCook, Hercules Shoemaker, Spittal, Old Machar   At Falkirk and
Culloden

McCrody, James Miltown of Shenval

MacDonald, Alexander Delnabo, Banffshire

McDonald, Alexander Servant, Cairnwhelp, Aberdeenshire

McDonald, Alexander Servant, Minmore

McDonald, Alexander Merchant, Aberdeen   In prison in Aberdeen   The
Aberdeen Journal records that "on 21 September 1772, died after a
short illness, Alexander McDonald, Merchant of Aberdeen, who
besides an inflexible honesty possessed a large stock of true but
harmless wit and good humour, which, as it afforded much pleasure to
others, contributed not a little to his own support under many
hardships he suffered in the course of his life."

McDonald, Angus Servant, Pitchaish
McDonald, Coll Badivochal
McDonald, Donald Balintomb, Kirkmichael
McDonald, George Nether Achregnie
McDonald, George Aberdeen Monaltrie's Regiment, prisoner at Culloden
McDonald, James Inveraven, Banffshire
McDonald, James Middle Achdregnie
McDonald, James Banff Transported 20 March 1747
McDonald, James Badivochal
McDonald, Jane Strathbogie Followed Clanranald's Regiment
McDonald, John Auchriachan
McDonald, John Born 1723, resident in Stradoun Banffshire Transported
31 March 1747 from London to Barbados in *Frere*
McDonald, Joseph Born 1720, weaver, Morayshire Transported 5 May
1747 from Liverpool to Leeward Islands in *Veteran*, but the ship was
attacked off Antigua by a French privateer from Martinique The
Governor of Martinique refused English demands to hand the
prisoners back, and granted the request of 10 to be sent to France
possibly to negotiate for others
McDonald, Owen Transported 30 Mar 1747 from London to Barbados in
Frere
McDonald, Peter Tomintoul
McDonald, Robert Tarravan, Banffshire
McDonald, Ronald Servant at Brick-kilns, Old Machar
McDonald, Thomas Messenger, in the Tolbooth
McDonald, William Piper, Portsoy
McDonald, William Tailor, Tarravan
McDougall, Daniel In the Tolbooth, Aberdeen
McGee, Hugh Sailor Aberdeen Lurking after Culloden
McGinnis (or McInnes), Thomas Labourer, of Banffshire and prisoner at
Carlisle on 30 December 1745, and tried at York in October 1746
where he was executed on 8 November 1746
McGlashan, William Horsehirer, Strathbogie, Aberdeenshire Lurking after
Culloden
McGrath, Alexander Fodderletter
McGregor, Captain, of Inverenzie, Glengairn Grandson of Malcolm
McGregor of Inverenzie, believed to have been wounded at Culloden,
and afterwards killed by some English soldiers when they saw him
move as told by Patrick Fleming, who escaped notice
McGregor, Duncan Farmer, Tarland, Aberdeenshire Transported 24 Feb
1747 from Liverpool to Virginia in *Gildart*, arrived Port North Potomac,
Maryland, 5 Aug 1747.
McGrigor, Alexander Bellachnochlan, Avenside
McGrigor, Alexander Workman, Loanhead, Old Machar
McGrigor, Duncan Ensign in Monaltrie's Regiment, Aberdeen Prisoner at
Culloden, acquitted
McGrigor, Evan Candelmore
McGrigor, John Wester Gaulrig

34

McGrigor, Malcolm Achnakyle, Banffshire
McGrigor, Roy Delnabo. Deserter
McGrigor, William Findran. Killed
McGurman, John Wester Gaulrig.
McHardie, William Glen of Auchriachan
McIntosh, Alexander Tacksman in Elrig   Captain   Born 1727
    Transported 31 Mar 1747 from London to Barbados in *Frere*
McIntosh, Duncan   Born 1728, husbandman, Dyke, Morayshire
    Transported 20 March 1747 from London to Jamaica in *St George* or
    Carteret, arrived Jamaica 1747
McIntosh, John Easter Inverourie, Banffshire
McKay, Donald Servant, Fochabers, Moray.   Went to England with the
    Jacobites Killed.
McKay, Hugh Formerly Cook to the Duke of Gordon   Prisoner in Banff
McKay, John Merchant, Balno, Glenlivet
McKay, Neil Tidesman, Aberdeen   Dismissed from his post for being
    concerned in the Rebellion
McKay, Robert Nether Clashmore
McKay, Robert Bellachnochlan, Avenside
McKay, Thomas Born 1700 in Banff   Woodturner in Glenmoriston,
    Invernessshire Transported 20 March 1747
McKenzie, Donald Mason, Strathbogie, Aberdeenshire   Lurking after
    Culloden
McKenzie, Kenneth Servant, Dell
McKenzie, John Merchant, Dalmore, Banffshire
McKenzie, John Banffshire   Prisoner
McKenzie, John Surgeon, Elgin   Surgeon to Jacobites and very active
    Said to be in Edinburgh after Culloden
McKenzie, Lewis Born 1726, joiner, resident in Elgin, Morayshire
    Transported April 1747 from Tilbury to Jamaica in *St George* or
    Carteret, arrived Jamaica 1747
McKenzie, Thomas Botriphnie, Banffshire
McKenzie, William Born 1711   Resident in Banff   Bore arms
    Transported 1747
Mackie, Alexander Servant, Byers, Banff   Lurking after Culloden
Mackie, Alexander Servant, Keith, Banffshire   Lurking after Culloden
Mackie, Daniel Born 1729, labourer, resident in Morayshire   Transported 5
    May 1747 from Liverpool to Leeward Islands in *Veteran*, but the ship
    was attacked off Antigua by a French privateer from Martinique   The
    Governor of Martinique refused English demands to hand the
    prisoners back, and granted the request of 10 to be sent to France
    possibly to negotiate for others
Mackie, Peter A farmer's son, Midbelty, Kincardine O'Neil
McLaghlan, George Calier, Banffshire.
McLaghlan, James Prisoner in Carlisle
McLaghlan, John Prisoner in Carlisle.
McLaughlan, John Badivochal.   Labouring man, aged 69

McLaughlan, Peter Born 1707, weaver, Fochabers, Morayshire Transported 22 Apr 1747 from Liverpool to Virginia in *Johnson*, arrived Port Oxford, Maryland, 5 Aug 1747

McLea, Alexander Upper Downan, Banffshire

McLea, Allan Badiglashean

McLea, James Carloch, Morinsh

McLea, John Clagan, Glenlivet

McLea, Robert Coull, Banffshire

McLea, William Souie, Glenlivet

McLean, John Servant to James Tower, Ferryhill, Aberdeen

McPherson, Alexander Blarchybeg

McPherson, Alexander Milton of Auchriachan

McPherson, Donald "Brachachy"

McPherson, James Born 1725, labourer, resident of Aberdeen Black hair, 5ft 7ins lusty well made Transported 5 May 2747 from Liverpool to Leeward Islands in *Veteran*, but the ship was attacked off Antigua by a French privateer from Martinique The Governor of Martinique refused English demands to hand the prisoners back, and granted the request of 10 to be sent to France possibly to negotiate for others

McPherson, John Eldridge, Cabrach

McPherson, John Auchriachan

McPherson, John Fodderletter

McPherson, Malcolm, sen Of Phonas, Banffshire A Captain

McPherson, Thomas Achnarrow, Glenlivet

McRae, Alexander Described in Lord Rosebery's List of Rebels as "An Idler - Banff A Lieutenant "

McRobie, William Tomachork, Banffshire

McRobie, William Morinsch Killed

McWilliam, John Croughly

McWillie, David Auchriachan, in the Glens

McWillie, James Servant, Croughly, deserted from the King's army

Maine, John Born 1725 Fisher of Footdee, prisoner in Aberdeen Transported 22 Apr 1747 from Liverpool to Virginia in *Johnson*, arriving Port Oxford, Maryland 5 Aug 1747

Mair, James Servant, Strathbogie, Aberdeenshire Lurking after Culloden

Mair, John Whitefisher, Footdee Prisoner in Aberdeen

Mair, William Farmer, Blackhall, Strachan Killed at Culloden

Maitland, Mr John Non-jurant Minister, Caraldston (Careston) Originally from the Parish of Forgue in Aberdeenshire, the grandson of John Maitland, Minister of Inverkeithny, who died in 1698 leaving three sons Son of James Maitland, the eldest son, born in 1719 after his father's deposition Said to have administered Holy Communion to the dying Lord Strathallan, in oatmeal and whisky He escaped and lived for many years in France, dying in Edinburgh at an extreme old age at the end of 18th century

Malcolm, William Weaver, Keith, Banffshire Lurking after Culloden

Man, Alexander Servant, Slioch, Aberdeenshire Hired out

Marnoch, Alexander Born 1 May 1720, St Nicholas, son of John Marnoch and Janet Barnet. 26 years old, 5ft 4.5ins, brown hair, thick set Shoemaker, Aberdeen Transported 5 May 1747 from Liverpool to Leeward Islands in *Veteran*, but the ship was attacked off Antigua by a French privateer from Martinique. The Governor of Martinique refused English demands to hand the prisoners back, and granted the request of 10 to be sent to France possibly to negotiate for others
Marr, Alexander Butcher, Aberdeen Prisoner in Aberdeen
Marr, David Butcher, Aberdeen. Lurking after Culloden.
Marr, John Aberdeen. Prisoner at Carlisle. Truned King's evidence
Marr, Robert Butcher, Aberdeen
Marr, Robert Wright, Aberdeen Tidesman for the Jacobites
Marr, Thomas Mason, Banff.
Martha (or Matthew), Walter Gight, Aberdeenshire
Martin, Alexander Candelmore.
Martin, George Tomaclagan, Glenlivet
Martin, John Farmer, Gordon's Mill, Aberdeen Entered in Register of Merchants and Trade Burgess of Aberdeen in 1732 A prisoner in the Tolbooth of Aberdeen in May 1746 Taken to Carlisle, and acquitted on 19 Sept 1746 after trial
Martin, John Born 1705, stocking weaver, Stonhaven, Kincardineshire Transported 31 Mar 1747 from London to Jamaica in *St George* or *Carteret*, arrived Jamaica 1747
Mason, James Aberdeen Prisoner at Aberdeen
Mason, John Born 1699 Wright, Aberdeen Transported 20 Mar 1747 from Tilbury
Mason, John Whitefisher, Aberdeen
Mason, John Barber, Aberdeen Son of William Mason and Helen Mouat, born 29 June 1727, "18 years old, 5ft 3ins, brown hair and well looking" Transported 5 May 1747 from Liverpool to Leeward Islands in *Veteran*, but the ship was attacked off Antigua by the French, who released all prisoners in Martinique June 1747
Massie, Robert Turriff
Masson, John Whitefisher in Footdee
Matheson, Alexander Labourer, Old Rayne
Matheson, David Tailor, Strathbogie, Aberdeenshire Hired out by the inhabitants. Lurking after Culloden
Matheson, David Labourer, Old Rayne
Maver, James Son of William Maver, Turriff, Aberdeenshire Ran express with the Laird of Grant's letter to the Laird of Macleod Taken prisoner after Culloden
Maver, William Ale Seller, Turriff Father of James Maver
Melvin, Alexander Servant to William Menzies of Pitfoddels
Melvin, Alexander Prisoner in Aberdeen
Melvin, William Prisoner in Aberdeen.
Mensat, John Weaver, Achdregnie, Banffshire
Menzies, Alexander Prisoner in Aberdeen.

Menzies, Alexander Fifth son of William Menzies of Pitfodels, born in 1723 He went to Ratisbon from 1735 to 1738, and returned in November of that year with his youngest brother, James He died at Auchintoul in 1799, aged 76

Menzies, David Fourth son of William Menzies of Pitfodels, born in 1722, he was at the Scots College in Ratisbon with his brothers, William and Alexander from 1735 to 1738 Went into England and was present at Culloden, eventually escaping to France

Menzies, Gilbert, yr of Pitfodels Eldest son of William Menzies of Pitfodels and his wife Mary, eldest daughter of John Urquhart of Meldrum, born 1712 Present at Prestonpans, England, Falkirk and Culloden, he escaped to France He died before 1756, with no record of a marriage

Menzies, James Sixth and youngest son of William Menzies of Pitfodels, born 1725 In November 1738 he went with his brother Alexander to Ratisbon Fought throughout the whole Rising, and escaped Culloden ultimately to France Known to be still alive in 1772

Menzies, John Second son of William Menzies of Pitfodels, born in 1718 When aged 8 he accompanied his elder brother Gilbert to the Scots College at Douai He went into England with the Jacobites, and was present at Culloden In 1755 he married Marion, daughter of William Maxwell of Kirkconnell, by whom he had a son He died in Aberdeen in March 1756 His wife died at Nancy, Lorraine in May 1776

Menzies, William Third son of William Menzies of Pitfodels born in 1721 He accompanied his two younger brothers, David and Alexander to the Scots College at Ratisbon in July 1735 ADC to Lord Pitsligo, he went to England with the Prince and escaped after Culloden and via Sweden he eventually arrived in France

Mercer, Thomas, of Auchnacant Son of James Mercer, Merchant, Aberdeen He escaped after Culloden and wandered the country for some considerable time, changing his clothes as a disguise He escaped to France and lived in Paris His wife, Katherine Arbuthnot predeceased him in 1749, leaving two sons, David and James He died in 1770

Mercer, Thomas Son of Robert Mercer of Aldie, Cornet in Lord Nairne's Regiment A refugee in Sweden after Culloden

Merns, Alexander Labourer, Insch

Merry, George Aberdeenshire At Culloden

Michie, John West Achmore, Glenrinnes

Middleton, Alexander Servant Prisoner at Carlisle, transported

Middleton, James Labourer, Tilphoody, Aboyne

Middleton, James Banffshire At Culloden

Middleton, James Bellandy, dead

Middleton, Robert Porter, Fraserburgh, carried letters

Middleton, Samuel Pressed man for Pitfoddels Company

Middleton, Samuel Labourer, Tilabooty, Coull Lurking after Culloden

Middleton, William Labourer, Tilabooty, Cowl, Aberdeen Assisted the Jacobites but did not fight with them

Mill, Andrew Servant to a farmer in Tullycairn

Mill, George Labourer, Upper Torie, Nigg. Lurking after Culloden.

Mill, John Labourer, Longside. Prisoner in Chester.

Mill, William Merchant, Ellon, "made great rejoicings at rebels' success "

Miller, William Inchnacape, Banffshire. House burnt.

Million, Alexander Shoemaker, Loughtoun, Banchory.

Milln, William Aberdeen Prisoner at Culloden

Mills, William Born 1725 Servant, Aberdeen 5ft 3ins, sandy hair, healthy, well made. Transported 5 May 1747 from Liverpool to Leeward Islands in *Veteran*, but the ship was attacked off Antigua by a French privateer from Martinique The Governor of Martinique refused English demands to hand the prisoners back, and granted the request of 10 to be sent to France possibly to negotiate for others

Miln, James Pitfoddels

Milne (or Mill), Andrew Tailor, Banff Aged 17, 5ft 7.25ins, brown hair, brown complexion, slender, thin At Carlisle garrison Transported 5 May 1747 from Liverpool to Leeward Islands in *Veteran*, but the ship was attacked off Antigua by a French privateer from Martinique The Governor of Martinique refused English demands to hand the prisoners back, and granted the request of 10 to be sent to France possibly to negotiate for others

Milne, George Bridgend, Turriff

Milne, George Son of George Milne, Innkeeper, Turriff, Aberdeenshire Lurking after Culloden

Milne, George Croft of Inverlochy House burnt

Milne, John Servant, Boadford, Banff Lurking after Culloden

Milne, William Turriff

Milne, William Son to James Milne, Mason, Turriff, Aberdeenshire Lurking after Culloden.

Mitchell, Alexander Banff Born 1719. Servant to Stewart of Bog Transported 31 Mar 1747 from London to Barbados in *Frere*

Mitchell, Alexander Farmer, Cairnwhelp, Aberdeenshire

Mitchell, George Workman, Loanhead, Old Machar. Prisoner in Aberdeen

Mitchell, George Old Machar, Aberdeen Transported 24 Feb 1747 from Liverpool to Virginia in *Gildart*, arrived Port North Potomac, Maryland, 5 Aug 1747

Mitchell, James Arnhall, Aberdeenshire Executed at Carlisle

Mitchell, James Weaver, Keith, Banffshire Lurking after Culloden

Mitchell, James Labourer, Aberdeen Forcibly carried along with the army

Mitchell, James Workman, Loanhead Old Machar Prisoner in Aberdeen

Mitchell, Robert Barber, Aberdeen A Sergeant

Mitchell, Walter Born 1728 Under-tenant in the parish of King Edward in Aberdeenshire. His mother kept an alehouse He was a student at Aberdeen University (aged 17) but left in autumn 1745 for fear of Gordon of Glenbucket's men, who were searching for recruits He was later taken by force from his mother's house, and given a commission under Lord Pitsligo Sentenced to death, but reprieved, he was eventually transported on Mr Samuel Smith's ship in Sept 1748

Mitchell, William Farmer, Piltachy, Ellon

Moir, Charles Shipmaster, Aberdeen   Younger brother of James Moir of Stoneywood   After Culloden he went into hiding, and got to Gottenburg   On 1 Aug 1747 Patrick Byres wrote to tell him to buy a place as a Burgher in Rotterdam which "would cost a triffling 15 or 20 francs or a Burgher in Gottenburg, which might be better as the Dutch might soon be at war with the French "   Moir seems to have acted on this advice

Moir, Colin Badivochal

Moir, Donald Dinnet   Wounded at Culloden

Moir, James Shoemaker, Old Aberdeen   Assisted in unloading the ships

Moir, James, of Stoneywood 4th Laird of Stoneywood, the eldest son of James Moir, 3rd of Stoneywood and his wife Jean Erskine of Pittodrie He was born in 1710 and married, at Ardross in 1740, his cousin, Margaret Mackenzie of Ardross, by whom he had 15 children, most of whom died in infancy, except Charles (born 1752) killed in America, and two daughers, Jane and Maria   He was a very active recruiter for the Jacobite cause   His house was occuped by Cumberland's men, and their officer was nursed back to health by Mrs Moir   The young Englishman did not forget his debt, and after the Battle of Culloden she received a note wrapped around a stone, thrown though her window, bearing the words, "Stoneywood is safe "   He eventually escaped to Gottenburgh where his wife joined him, becoming a merchant there   Prince Charles recommended him to the King of Sweden and he became a naturalized Swedish subject   He eventually returned to Stoneywood   He died 29 Sept 1784 aged 74, leaving a widow and two daughters   Mrs Moir died 6 Dec 1805 at the advanced age of 96

Moir, John Labourer, Auchmore, Midmar, Aberdeen   Lurking after Culloden.

Moir, William, of Lonmay Eldest son of James Moir, 2nd of Stoneywood, by his second wife, Jean Abernethy of Mayen, widow of William Moir of Scotstown   Married daughter of John Fullarton of Dudwick, by whom he had one son, William and two daughters, Isabella and Catherine Factor to the Countess of Erroll, Bowence, Cruden, at Nethermiln, Cruden   Died 24 May 1752

Moir, William Sailor, Invernetty, Peterhead   Second son of William Moir, merchant, Aberdeen, he survived the Rising   He married Jean, daughter of Colonel Lewis Hay, who died 25 Dec 1770 aged 49   He died 22 March 1778

Moll, John Braehead, Aberdeen

Montgomery, Peter Saddler, Fochabers, Moray   Lurking after Culloden

Montgomery, Robert Beggar, Old Aberdeen

More, John Auchmore, Midmar

More, John, jun Auchmore, Midmar

More, Peter Knockando, Banffshire

Morgan, Charles Servant, Ellon

Morgan, Charles Born 1729, barber, resident Elgin, Morayshire   5ft 4ins, brown hair and well made   Served in Glenbucket's regiment and taken at Carlisle   Transported 5 May 1747 from Liverpool to Leeward Islands in *Veteran*, but the ship was attacked off Antigua by a French privateer from Martinique   The Governor of Martinique refused English demands to hand the prisoners back, and granted the request of 10 to be sent to France possibly to negotiate for others

Morgan, George Aberdeen   Prisoner

Morgan, Patrick (or Peter) Foginell, Aberdeenshire. Transported 22 Apr 1747 from Liverpool to Virginia in *Johnson*, arriving Port Oxford, Maryland, 5 Aug 1747

Morgan, Peter Fodderletter

Morise, James Labouring servant, Ellon

Morison, Alexander Sailor, Fraserburgh   Concerned in apprehending Captain Alexander Grant going to join Lord Loudoun at Inverness

Morison, Alexander A farmer's son, Knockieburn, Turriff, Banffshire   Lurking after Culloden

Morison, John Servant, Auchterless, Aberdeenshire   Lurking after Culloden

Morison, John Banffshire   At Culloden

Morison, William Servant, Dorlaithers, Aberdeenshire   Lurking after Culloden

Morrison, Alexander Farmer, Muckle Colp, Aberdeenshire   Lurking after Culloden

Mosman, Thomas Writer, Aberdeen   His wife was Elizabeth, daughter of James Sandilands, 3rd of Craibston, and possibly sister to Robert and Bartholemew

Muir, Alexander East Pitchaish, Surgeon

Muir, Robert Writer, Aberdeen   Hussar

Mull, George Aberdeenshire   Prisoner

Munzie, Alexander Imprisoned in Aberdeen

Murdo, William Shoemaker's servant, Aberdeen   One of those who brought Spanish arms from Peterhead

Murdoch, George Farmer, Reekie, Alford   Prisoner at Culloden

Murdoch, ... Brother of George Murdoch, Alford   Killed at Culloden

Murray, John Aberdeen   Glenbucket's Regiment, in Carlisle, transported

Murray, Peter Servant to William Coutts, prisoner in Aberdeen   Had to find caution for good behaviour

Mutch, George Labourer, Little Arnage   Joined after Falkirk

Mutch, John Labourer, Ellon. Joined after Falkirk

Nairn, Thomas Born 1712   Chapman, Strathdon   Transported 19 Mar 1747 from London to Jamaica in *St George* or *Carteret*, arriving Jamaica 1747

Neilson, John (or James) Labourer, Aberdeen. Born 1721   5ft 5ins, black hair, swarthy, slender. At Carlisle   Transported 5 May 1747 from Liverpool to Leeward Islands in *Veteran*, but the ship was attacked off Antigua by a French privateer from Martinique   The Governor of

Martinique refused English demands to hand the prisoners back, and granted the request of 10 to be sent to France possibly to negotiate for others

Nicol, Walter Prisoner in Aberdeen

Nicoll, George Weaver, Aberdeen   Born 10 Sept 1721, Old Machar, son of Andrew Nicoll and Margaret Mitchell   26 years old, 5ft 7ins, brown hair, strong, well made   At Carlisle   Transported 5 May 1747 from Liverpool to Leeward Islands in Veteran, but the ship was attacked off Antigua by a French privateer from Martinique   The Governor of Martinique refused English demands to hand the prisoners back, and granted the request of 10 to be sent to France possibly to negotiate for others

Nicoll, ... great grandfather of the Rev Harry Nicoll, minister of Auchindoir, father of Dr Robertson Nicoll

Nicholls, Isabel Aberdeen   Followed Pitsligo's Regiment

Nicholson, Alexander Inveraven

Nicholson, William Servant, Strathbogie, Aberdeenshire   Hired out   Lurking after Culloden

Nicholson, George Aberdeenshire   Prisoner

Nicholson, Gilbert Aberdeenshire   Prisoner

Niddray, Alexander Weaver, Fraserburgh

Nisbet, William Farmer, Waterside, Slains   Declared he had been obliged to take up arms after being threatened by the Countess of Erroll, and later gave evidence against her

Niven (or Nivie), James Merchant, Aberdeen   Taken from Aberdeen Tolbooth to Carlisle, tried and executed

Niven, John Son of James Niven, merchant, Aberdeen   Imprisoned as a boy with his father at Carlisle   He became rich in the tobacco trade and lived in a house in the Ghaistrow (Ghost Row) called Thornton Court

Norald, Adam Labourer, Old Meldrum

Ochterlony, David Servant to Andrew Skene, Surgeon   Prisoner, Aberdeen

Ogg, William Labourer, Muryhall, Aboyne   Lurking after Culloden

Ogilvie, Alexander Shoemaker, Corridoun, Banffshire   Lurking after Culloden

Ogilvie, Alexander, of Auchiries Son of James Ogilvie of Auchiries and Margaret Strachan, his wife, born in 1723   Surviving the Rising, he married in 1742, Mary, daughter of George Cumine of Pitullie, and sister of William Cumine   By her he had one son, George, who succeeded to Acuhiries, and a daughter Margaret   After the death of his first wife he married Barbara, daughter of Thomas Robertson of Downiehills   He died 3 March 1791, aged 68

Ogilvie, David Prisoner in the Tolbooth, Aberdeen

Ogilvie, John Born 1728, twin to William   Younger brother of Alexander Son to James Ogilvie of Auchiries   He survived the Rising and ultimately went abroad and became a doctor   He died in St Eustatia, leaving no issue

42

Ogilvie, Patrick Servant, Ardoch, Banffshire. Lurking in house of Patrick Duff, Speyside

Ogilvie, Walter Writer in Banff Went with the Highland army to England A prisoner in Carlisle, he was conveyed to London where he was tried at age 19 With a Macdonald and Nicholson in Highland dress and Ogilvie in Lowland dress, they were first hung, cut down alive, their intestines and heart taken out and burnt before their faces in a fire, and their heads were cut off

Ogilvie, William Merchant, Aberdeen Lurking after Culloden.

Ogilvie, William Born 1728, twin to John Ogilvie, son of James Ogilvie of Auchiries. He survived the Rising and went to America and settled in Virginia where he died in 1750 leaving no issue

Oldman, James Aldie, Cruden Joined after Preston

Oliphant, Charles Excise Officer, Aberdeen, and servant to Lord Lyon Admitted to New Gaol, Southward, alone, on 21 Aug 1746 Present at Falkirk, Stirling and Culloden He was reprieved but still in jail on 15 Aug 1747, where he complained that his wife was refused access to him unless she pay 1 shilling to gaolor He was banished to America in Sept 1748, and went there in the following year

Ord, James Wigmaker, Cullen, Banffshire One of the Hussars Lurking after Culloden

Panton, Alexander Innkeeper, Turriff Assisted in robbing James Paterson, carrier, Banff

Paterson, Alexander Labourer, Todlochy, Monymusk Lurking after Culloden.

Paterson, George Householder, New Durn, Banff

Paterson, Hercules Surgeon, Keith Involved in the Battle of Inverury, where he freely admitted lying in a ditch during the firing In July 1746 he was "lurking".

Paterson, James Banff Servant to Mergie

Paterson, Robert Labourer, Old Meldrum

Paterson, Robert Born 3 July 1728, Old Macher, Aberdeen, son of Abraham Paterson and Elspet Shepherd Hosier, Aberdeen, 19 years old, 5ft 5ins, slender, well made Known to have been taken after the Siege of Carlisle Transported 5 May 1747 from Liverpool to Leeward Islands in *Veteran*, but the ship was attacked off Antigua by a French privateer from Martinique The Governor of Martinique refused English demands to hand the prisoners back, and granted the request of 10 to be sent to France possibly to negotiate for others

Paton, George Journeyman shoemaker, Aberdeen Was concerned in some mobs, for which he was apprehended, but afterwards admitted to bail

Paton, William Tomintoul

Pattison, Robert Aberdeen Carlisle garrison

Peirie, Alexander Labourer, Old Meldrum

Perrie, John Elgin. Volunteer. Lurking after Culloden

Petrie, James Sheriff-Substitute, Aberdeen An advocate apprenticed to Thomas Burnet in 1722. In hiding after the Rising, he resumed his practice at the Aberdeen bar on 14 April 1748   He married Elizabeth Jamieson (d Aberdeen 21 March 1770, aged 70), and had one son and one daughter   He died 19 Oct 1763

Petrie, Lewis Servant to Dr Forbes, in prison in Aberdeen

Petrie, William Portsoy

Philip, William Weaver, Aberdeen

Pierie, Charles Son to Alexander Peirie at Miln Auchter, Ellon   Joined after Preston

Pirie, Andrew Labourer, Ellon

Pirie, John Servant to Dorlaithers

Pitsligo, Lord A prominent Jacobite in both the '15 and '45, about whom much has been written   Alexander Forbes, 4th and last Lord Forbes of Pitslig was the only son and heir of Alexander and his wife, Sophia Erskine, daughter of the Earl of Mar, born 24 May 1678   He was involved in both uprisings   He married firstly, Rebecca, daughter of John Morton, by whom he had a son John   She died in 1731   He married, secondly, in September 1731, Elizabeth Allen, and English lady who died without issue 1759   She had been companion of his first wife   He was sought for many years, and died 21 December 1762 aged 84

Quin, Alexander Fochabers

Ramsay, Alexander Merchant, Rosehearty, Pitsligo   He went to England with the Highland army   He had a sister, Barbara Ramsay

Ramsay, Charles sen Merchant, Aberdeen   Prisoner in Tolbooth

Ramsay, Charles jun Merchant, Aberdeen   Prisoner in Tolbooth

Ramsay, George Surrendered at Carlisle, 30 Dec 1745 and carried to London   Although it is claimed he was a wheelwright and farmer, a petition was surprisingly made on his behalf by the Venetian ambassador   He had a wife and children, but he was eventually transported on 21 July 1748 from London

Ramsay, James Servant, Boathole, Durris   At Falkirk and lurking after Culloden

Ramsay, Kenneth Labourer, Old Meldrum

Ramsay, William Labourer, Loanhead, Rayne

Ranald, Francis Born 1/31   Herd in Strathbogie, Aberdeenshire   Transported 31 March 1747 from London to Barbados in *Frere*

Rannie, John Labourer, Old Meldrum

Rattray, John Balno, Banffshire

Reid, Alexander Aberdeen   Escaped from Edinburgh Castle

Reid, Donald Labourer, Inver, Braemar   At Falkirk and lurking after Culloden

Reid (or Read), George Born 29 May 1716, Deskford, Banffshire, son of Walter Reid   Labourer   5ft 4 5ins, dark visage, strong, healthy   In Carlisle   Transported from Liverpool to Leeward Islands in *Veteran*, but the ship was attacked off Antigua by a French privateer from Martinique   The Governor of Martinique refused English demands to hand the prisoners back, and granted the request of 10 to be sent to France possibly to negotiate for others

Reid, James Aberdeen.   In Carlisle

Reid, James Wright, Aboyne.   Forced by Gordon of Blelack

Reid, John Stabler, Aberdeen   At Culloden.

Reid, Robert Mason, Aberdeen

Reid, Robert Aberdeen.   Executed at Carlisle.   Was in arms in a mob on Prince of Wales' birthday   Recruited men in Aberdeen

Reid, Robert, jun of Barra Merchant   Son of Sir Alexander Reid, 2nd Baronet of Barra, and his wife Aganes, eldest daughter of Sir Alexander Ogilvie of Forglen   They had four sons, Alexander James, Robert and William, and two daughters, Helen and Barbara   Apprentice to a merchant in Aberdeen

Reid, Robert Servant, Charlestown of Aboyne   At Falkirk and lurking after Culloden

Reid, Robert Mason, Aberdeen

Reid, William Aberdeen   In the Tolbooth

Reid, William Tidesman, Aberdeen   Dismissed from his post for being concerned in the Rising

Reith, Alexander Tailor, Gateside, Upper Banchory   Lurking after Culloden.

Reoch, Alexander Gaulrig

Reoch, Alexander Cordwainer, Aberdeen   In London in custody of Carrington, Messenger   An evidence

Reoch, Donald Elrig, Kirkmichael

Reoch, James Candelmore, Banffshire

Reoch, John Wester Fodderletter

Reynolds, Francis Herd in Strathbogie

Reynoldson, (or Rannoldson) James Born 1722, weaver, Fetternear, Kindardineshire   Transported 31 Mar 1747 from London to Jamaica in *St George* or *Carteret*, arrived Jamaica 1747

Rhind, John Brewer, Findhorn   Assisted in plundering Findhorn

Riach, John Servant to Monaltrie, and evidence against him

Richy, John Horse hirer, Old Aberdeen

Richard, William Aberdeen   In Carlisle

Ritchy, Andrew Horsehirer, Old Aberdeen

Robb, Elizabeth Born 1712   A knitter, Aberdeen, 35 years old, 4ft 11ins, brown, thick set   Transported 5 May 1747 from Liverpool to Leeward Islands in *Veteran*, but the ship was attacked off Antigua by a French privateer from Martinique.   The Governor of Martinique refused English demands to hand the prisoners back, and granted the request of 10 to be sent to France possibly to negotiate for others

Robb, James Late servant to Sheriff Clerk, Aberdeen, at Aberdeen

Robertson, Alexander Chapman, in Rubislaw

Robertson, Alexander Aberdeen, in Tolbooth

Robertson, Alexander Labourer, Clintarty, Birse   At Falkirk and Culloden

Robertson, Charles Balmlagan (Balanallen, Avenside)

Robertson, James Servant, Wintertown, Banff   Lurking after Culloden

Robertson, John Wright, Aberdeen.

Robertson, John Labourer, Mickle Wartle, Rayne

Robertson, Patrick Servant, Findlater, Banff

Robertson, Patrick Servant, Findhorn, Banffshire   Lurking after Culloden

Robertson, Peter Piper, Fochabers, Moray

Robertson, William Born 1727, weaver Spynie, Morayshire, 5ft 3 75ins, dark hair well made   Transported 5 May 1747 from Liverpool to Leeward Islands in *Veteran*, but the ship was attacked off Antigua by a French privateer from Martinique   The Governor of Martinique refused English demands to hand the prisoners back, and granted the request of 10 to be sent to France possibly to negotiate for others

Robison, John Innkeeper, Strathbogie, Aberdeenshire, "hyr'd out by the inhabitants who were forced thereto by John Gordon of Avochie " Lurking after Culloden

Ronald, Alexander Bankhead of Auchindoir   Was at Culloden   His dirk is in the Museum at Clova

Rose, William Aberdeen   Gunner at Carlisle

Ross, Alexander Servant, Down, Banff   Lurking after Culloden

Ross, Alexander Farmer, Tullich, Glenmuick   Killed at Falkirk

Ross, Charles Formerly a soldier, Fochabers, Moray   Lurking after Culloden

Ross, Donald Aberdeenshire   Prisoner at Culloden

Ross, Francis, jun Surgeon. Old Meldrum

Ross, Hugh Labourer, Wester Clunie, Birss   At Falkirk and Culloden

Ross, Hugh Turner, Elgin   Volunteer   Lurking after Culloden

Ross, James Apprentice, Aberdeen   Ensign

Ross, James, sen Sheriff Officer. Aberdeen   A prisoner in Inverness

Ross, James, jun Son of James Ross. Senior, a boy, Aberdeen   Acted as a Drummer for the Jacobites, and was a prisoner in Inverness   Later described as "Cooper-Apprentice "   The two Rosses must have turned King's evidence to save their skins, as they would otherwise not have been taken to London, their services to the Jacobite army having been slight

Ross, John Sailor Aberdeen   Acted as an officer

Ross, John Butcher, Aberdeen   Prisoner

Ross, John Servant. Scalan

Ross, John Farmer. Forres

Ross, Robert Kirkhill, Tomintoul

Ross, Robert Gardener, Aberdeen   At Culloden

Ross, Robert Porter. Aberdeen   At Culloden, and prisoner in Aberdeen

Ross, Robert Tomnalinan, Glenlivet

Ross, Robert In Tolbooth, Aberdeen   Labourer

Ross, Thomas Wright. Mill of Collithie, Aberdeenshire

Ross, Thomas Born 1683   Labourer, Aberdeen   In Carlisle   Transported 22 Apr 1747 from Liverpool to Maryland in *Johnson*, arrived Port Oxford, Maryland, 5 Auig 1747

Ross, William Born 1711   Sailor, Aberdeenshire   5ft 3 5ins, dark hair, ruddy, well set, robust   In Carlisle   Transported 5 May 1747 from Liverpool to Leeward Islands in *Veteran*, but the ship was attacked off Antigua by a French privateer from Martinique   The Governor of

Martinique refused English demands to hand the prisoners back, and granted the request of 10 to be sent to France possibly to negotiate for others.

Ross, William Ruthven in Kirkmichael

Roy, Hugh Aberdeen   At Carlisle

Roy, John Aberdeen. At Carlisle, son of Hugh Roy

Roy, John Innkeeper, Cabrach   House burnt

Roy, John Servant, Turriff, Aberdeenshire   Lurking after Culloden

Roy-Grant, Peter Badinglashean, Ballindalloch.

Roy-Stuart, John Tombreac, Banffshire

Russel, Hugh Apprentice, Aberdeen   At the skirmish of Inverurie

Russell, David Born 1727   Glover, Aberdeen   Transported 22 Apr 1747 from Liverpool to Maryland in *Johnson*, arrived Port Oxford, Maryland, 5 Aug 1747.

Sandilands, Bartholomew Escaped to Bergen in 1746   From Bordeaux, son to the merchant   He was probably very young

Sandilands, Robert Writer, Aberdeen, of the Craibstone family   With the Jacobite army in Derby and subsequent retreat   After Culloden he was in Sweden along with Moir of Stoneywood and other Jacobites   Married Isabella, daughter of Patrick Byres of Tonley (she died without issue, having been killed by a fall from a carriage)

Sandison, Peter Labourer, Glenmuick

Sangster, Charles Lonmay   Accidentally shot, March 1746   Buried at Essil

Sangster, William Labourer, Bullers of Buchan, Cruden

Sanyson, Peter Labourer, Tullich, Glemuck   At Falkirk and lurking after Culloden

Scot, Alexander Labourer, Turnilove, Cruden

Scot, William Servant, Carnousie, Banffshire   Lurking after Culloden

Scot, William Farmer, Blackwater, St Fergus

Scott, George Town Clerk of Inverurie   Son of George Scott and Margaret Ferguson, eldest daughter of Baillie Walter Ferguson of Inverurie   He died at the Mill of Aden in 1789   He was in the Tolbooth Aberdeen from 6 April 1746 to 6 March 1747

Scott, John Sailor, Aberdeen. Son of Robert Scott, deceased, merchant in Edinburgh   His mother married Rev George Law   He was very active though very young.   He was a prisoner in the Tolbooth of Aberdeen, Carlisle and York Castle, and later after a reprieve, transported to Antigua on 8 May 1747

Scroggie, William Age 15, Aberdeenshire   Prisoner at Inverness

Scroggy, Robert Servant-lad, Eshly, Upper Banchory   Acted as Tidesman for the Jacobites in Aberdeen   At Culloden

Shand, Andrew Husbandman, Banff

Shand, William Servant, Corsairtly, Banffshire   Taken at prisoner at Culloden.

Shand, William Husbandman, Banff

Shanks, Alexander Chapel of Garioch, Aberdeenshire

Sharp, William This 16 year old boy belonged to Banffshire, the great-grandson of the famous Archbishop of Sharp, murdered outside St Andrews His father was Sir William Sharp of Stonyhill (then deceased) and Margaret Hamilton, daughter of Mr Philip Hamilton of Kilbrackmount He was baptised 28 January 1729 A free pardon was obtained, but he had succeeded in escaping before this news reached him

Sharp, William Born 1729, aged 18, labourer, Aberdeen, 5ft 5 5ins, brown hair, slender At Carlisle Transported 5 May 1747 from Liverpool to Leeward Islands in *Veteran*, but the ship was attacked off Antigua by a French privateer from Martinique The Governor of Martinique refused English demands to hand the prisoners back, and granted the request of 10 to be sent to France possibly to negotiate for others

Shaw, Duncan Eldest son of James Shaw Factor to the Earl of Airlie

Shaw, James Daldownie, Gairnside Son of Duncan Shaw, portioner of Crathienaird Came unscathed through the whole Rising He married three times, first a daughter of John Young of Birkhill or Birkhall, by whom he had 2 sons, Duncan and John His second wife was a daughter of Farquhar of Auchterfoull in the parish of Coull, and by her he had 4 daughters The third wife was Margaret, daughter of Donald Farquharson of Micras, by whom he had 2 daughters and 2 sons, Donald and Alexander He died at Inverey on 19 Feb 1768

Shaw, John Fiddler, Aberdeen Prisoner at Aberdeen

Shaw, John Second son of James Shaw of Daldownie by his first wife He was an ardent Jacobite who came safely through the Rising

Sherrif, John Barber, Aberdeen Lurking after Culloden

Shives, Alexander Labourer, Old Meldrum

Sill, James Merchant Aberdeen Lurking after Culloden

Simpson, Adam Cottar, Glengerack Said to be hired out Lurking after Culloden

Simpson, James Servant lad in Charlestown, Aboyne At Falkirk and Culloden, but said to be forced out

Simpson, John Farmer, Auchinhove Lieutenant Was at the skirmish at Keith Lurking after Culloden

Simpson, John Bleacher, Grange

Simpson, John Merchant, Huntly, Officer of Hussars

Sinclair, Gilbert Keith Deserted Prisoner at Culloden

Sinclair, John Fiddler, Newmills of Boyne, Banffshire Prisoner at Banff

Skene, John Tailor, Turriff, Aberdeenshire Lurking after Culloden

Smart, John Servant to Adam Hay of Asleid, and evidence against him Prisoner at Tilbury

Smith, Alexander Labourer, Old Meldrum

Smith, Alexander Servant, Drindolo, Aberdeen

Smith, Alexander Labourer, Glentanar

Smith, Alexander Of Menie, Belhelvie Son of Patrick Smith of the Inveramsay family His mother was Elizabeth Kerr

Smith, Andrew, jun Inveramsay Born 1716, son of Patrick Smith and Elizabeth Kerr (d 1761, after her husband) Husbandman, near Old

Meldrum After his trial he was transported on 24 Feb 1747 from Liverpool to Virginia in *Gildart*, arriving Port North Potomac, Maryland, 5 Aug 1747.

Smith, Andrew Born 1726, husbandman in Old Meldrum, Aberdeenshire Transported 31 March 1747 from London to Barbados in *Frere*

Smith, Andrew Aberdeen Prisoner at Culloden Crichton's Regiment

Smith, Betty Prisoner in Aberdeen

Smith, Daniel Merchant, Aberdeen Shortly before the Rising he married Annie Gordon, connected with the Wardhouse family He was killed at Culloden.

Smith, David, jun of Inveramsay Eldest son of Patrick Smith of Inveramsay (d 1743) and Elizabeth Kerr His grandfather, John Smith died in 1750 aged nearly 100 He was exempted from the Act of Indemnity of 1747 His brothers were Alexander and Andrew and sisters, Helen, Clementina, Janet, Marjory and Rachel

Smith, Edward House carpenter, Banff Transported

Smith, Francis sen Servant, Charlestown, Aboyne At Culloden

Smith, Francis jun Servant, Charlestown, Aboyne At Culloden but said to be forced out

Smith, George Born 1723 Husbandman at Cairbulg Aberdeenshire Transported 31 Mar 1747 from London to Jamaica in *St George* or *Carteret*, arriving Jamaica 1747

Smith, George Farmer, Welcomin, Aberdeen

Smith, George Farmer, Upper Bridgend, Aberdeenshire Recruited men for Jacobites

Smith, James Prisoner at Culloden

Smith, James Writer in Edinburgh, Newmills of Boyne, Banffshire Lurking after Culloden

Smith, James Born 1688, aged 59 Workman, Loanhead, Old Machar Transported 31 Mar 1747 from London to Jamaica in *St George* or *Carteret*, arriving Jamaica 1747.

Smith, James Labourer, Old Deer

Smith, James Labourer, Old Meldrum

Smith, John Carter, Elgin. Very active in Rebellion At home after Culloden

Smith, John Merchant, Elgin Acted as storemaster for the Jacobites Lurking after Culloden

Smith, John Aberdeen Prisoner at Culloden

Smith, John Born 1726, aged 21, 5ft 4ins, brown hair, well made Goldsmith, Aberdeen Taken at Carlisle garrison Transported 5 May 1747 from Liverpool to Leeward Islands in *Veteran*, but the ship was attacked off Antigua by a French privateer from Martinique The Governor of Martinique refused English demands to hand the prisoners back, and granted the request of 10 to be sent to France possibly to negotiate for others.

Smith, John Labourer, Old Deer.

Smith, John Husbandman, Aberdeen. At Culloden

Smith, Peter Labourer, Auchlossan, Lumphanan Lurking after Culloden, but said to be forced out.

Smith, Robert Inverourie, Banffshire.

Smith, Robert Servant lad, Bridge Dy, Strachan   At Culloden.

Smith, William Labourer, Yonderton, Ellon

Smith, William Carrier, Keith, Banffshire   Hired out   Lurking after Culloden

Smith, William Banff   Pardoned on condition of enlistment

Smith, William Skinner, Forres

Soutar, John Labourer, Ellon, Aberdeenshire   Transported 22 Apr 1747 from Liverpool to Virginia in *Johnson*, arriving Port Oxford, Maryland, 5 Aug 1747

Spens, John Labourer, Miln of Botom, Insch

Steel, Alexander Tillytarmint, Banffshire

Steel, George Merchant, Aberdeen   Though very young, compelled some inhabitants of Aberdeen to go to Peterhead and help in bringing arms from a Spanish ship   He was a prisoner in Aberdeen in June 1746 and transferred to Carlisle   He was acquitted because of his surrender

Steil, James Merchant   In the Tolbooth, Aberdeen

Stephen, William Merchant, Elgin   "Remarkable for billating the Rebels on persons well affected to the Government"   At home after Culloden

Steuart, James Wigmaker, Turriff, Aberdeenshire   Lurking after Culloden

Steuart, William Journeyman baker, Turriff or Aberdeen   Prisoner in Aberdeen

Stewart, Alexander Aucholzie, Glenmuick   Eldest son of William Stewart of Aucholzie and his wife Euphame Farquharson, daughter of Harry Farquharson of Whitehouse, and sister of Harry Farquharson of Whitehouse Mill, who was killed at Culloden   Married Anna Gordon, only daughter of Robert Gordon of Corse 9 Jul 1714, and by her had two daughters, Margaret and Helen   He died in May 1746 of wounds received at Culloden

Stewart, David Born 1707   Resident of Banff   Prisoner at Carlisle   Transported 20 Mar 1747

Stewart, Duncan Aberdeen   Prisoner at Culloden

Stewart, James Major in Duke of Perth's regiment   10 years in his service, and described as valet, menial, servant or Chamberlain   Taken prisoner after Culloden, he was in New Gaol, Southward on 8 Aug 1746   Reprieved for having saved life of Major Bowles at Prestonpans, the brother of the late Major Bowles petitioned in his favour, and he received a free and unconditional pardon on 20 Aug 1747

Stewart, James Son of John Stewart, farmer in Borland   Present at Falkirk, Inverurie and Culloden, but not taken prisoner

Stewart, James In Aberdeen Tolbooth

Stewart, James Farmer, Strathbogie, Aberdeen

Stewart, James Captain, Aberdeen   Prisoner at Culloden

Stewart, John Born 1729   Labourer, Banff   Transported 5 May 1747 from Liverpool to Leeward Islands in *Veteran*, but the ship was attacked off Antigua by a French privateer from Martinique   The Governor of

Martinique refused English demands to hand the prisoners back, and granted the request of 10 to be sent to France possibly to negotiate for others

Stewart, John Aged 18, labourer, Aberdeen, 5ft 4.5ins, brown hair, well made, ruddy. Transported 5 May 1747 from Liverpool to Leeward Islands in *Veteran*, but the ship was attacked off Antigua by a French privateer from Martinique   The Governor of Martinique refused English demands to hand the prisoners back, and granted the request of 10 to be sent to France possibly to negotiate for others

Stewart, John Farmer, Borland, Glentanar, Aberdeenshire   He had three sons in the Rising.

Stewart, Joseph Son of John Stewart, farmer in Borland   Present at Falkirk, Inverurie and Culloden, but not taken prisoner

Stewart, Ludovick Representative, with his brother Robert, of Sir Walter Stewart of Strathaven and Glenlivet

Stewart, Peter Son of John Stewart, farmer in Borland   Present at Falkirk, Inverurie and Culloden, but not taken prisoner

Stewart, Robert Representative, with his brother Ludovick, of Sir Walter Stewart of Strathaven and Glenlivet   Severely wounded at Keith

Stivenson, James Servant, Edingight, Banffshire

Stodhart, William Innkeeper, Keith, Banffshire   Was a spy on the Royal Army, and conducted the Highlanders to attack the Campbells at Keith.   Lurking after Culloden

Stot, James Slater, Aberdeen   Lurking after Culloden

Strachan, James Workman, Loanhead, Old Machar   Lurking after Culloden

Strachan, James Born 1728   Student, educated Aberdeen University   Resident of Kincardineshire   Transported 24 Feb 1747 from Liverpool to Virginia in *Gildart*, arrived Port North Potomac, Maryland, 5 Aug 1747.

Strachan, James Extraordinary Tidesman, Aberdeen   Lurking after Culloden

Strachan, John A dyster, Aberdeen   In the Tolbooth

Strachan, William Clerk to the Customs, Aberdeen   Probably son of William Strachan, senior, merchant, Aberdeen, a keen Hanovarian   At Culloden   In 1748 he was in Paris

Stratton, James Born 1672, mason, resident in Morayshire   Transported 24 Apr 1747 from Liverpool to Virginia in *Johnson*, arriving Port Oxford, Maryland, 5 Aug 1747

Streethead, James Banff.   Prisoner at Carlisle

Stuart, Alexander Horsehirer, Strathbogie, Aberdeenshire

Stuart, Alexander Upper Achlichny, Kirkmichael

Stuart, Alexander Tacksman of Excise, Tomnavoulin, Glenlivet, an Ensign

Stuart, Allan Gaulrig, Banffshire

Stuart, Allan Newtown of Glenlivet

Stuart, Angus Farmer, Parkbeg, Banffshire   Ensign in Roy Stuart's Regiment.   Lurking after Culloden.

Stuart, Angus Dow Achnakyle, Banffshire.

Stuart, Donald Glack, Banffshire.

Stuart, Donald Findran, Tomintoul
Stuart, Donald Ruthven of Kirkmichael   Was at the rifling of Cullen House
Stuart, Donald Achnakyle, Kirkmichael
Stuart, Donald Glenconglass
Stuart, George Badivochal, Glenlivet
Stuart, Lewis Balachnockan, Deskie
Stuart, James East Inverourie, Avenside, Banffshire
Stuart, James Aberdeenshire, prisoner
Stuart, John Aberdeenshire, prisoner
Stuart, John Glenconglass
Stuart, John Findran, Tomintoul
Stuart, John Torbain, Kirkmichael
Stuart, John East Inverourie, Banffshire
Stuart, John Tomnavoulin
Stuart, John, jun Balachnockan, Deskie
Stuart, John Upper Achdregnie
Stuart, John (alias Dow) Upper Achdregnie
Stuart, John Delavorar
Stuart, Patrick Croughly
Stuart, Patrick Farmer, Tinninder   Captain   Lurking after Culloden
Stuart, Peter (or Patrick), yr of Tannachy Eldest son of George Stuart of
    Tannachy, Portgordon, who married Anne, daughter of Sir James
    Abercromby of Birkenbog (d Dec 1748)   Married to his cousin,
    Elizabeth (d 1806), younger daughter of Alexander Steuart of
    Auchlunkart   He died 21 Dec 1777 aged 50, leaving issue   George,
    Alexander Andrew, Harriet Mary, Elizabeth Margaret
Stuart, Peter (alias Dow) Badivochal, Glenlivet
Stuart, Peter Gentleman, Oxhill, Banff   Lurking after Culloden
Stuart, Robert Badivochal, Glenlivet
Stuart, Robert Downan, Deskie
Stuart, Robert Servant to Glenbucket
Stuart, Thomas Gardener to the Countess of Erroll, Gateside, Cruden
Stuart, William Bregach   A Captain and very active in raising men
Stuart, William Clashmore
Stuart, William Old Leek, Aberlour
Stuart, William West Achivaich
Stuart, William   Surrendered at Carlisle 30 Dec 1745 and tried in
    Southward   Possibly acquitted 19 Sept 1746
Suitor, John Labourer, Ellon
Sutherland, Alexander Wright, Fochabers, Moray   Lurking after Culloden
Sutherland, George Servant, Fochabers, Moray   Lurking after Culloden
Sutter, John Joiner, Ellon   Carlisle garrison, transported.
Symers, Alexander Gardener, Aberdeen   Was at Culloden
Taylor, James Shoemaker, Newmills of Boyn, Banffshire
Taylor, James Farmer, Pitmain, Banffshire
Taylor, John Aberdeenshire, prisoner

Taylor, John Born 1719, servant, resident Boharm, Banffshire Transported 22 April 1747 from Liverpool to Virginia in *Johnson*, arriving Port Oxford, Maryland, 5 Aug 1747

Taylor, Robert Labourer, Old Meldrum. Beat the drum and carried French colours before an officer who enlisted men

Taylor, William Croughly

Tailor, William Farmer's son, Dallachy, Banffshire. An Ensign, very active

Tervas, Alexander Merchant, Fraserburgh

Thain, James Servant to John Turras, Old Meldrum

Thain, John Mason, Strathbogie, Aberdeenshire, said to be hired out Lurking after Culloden

Thom, William Writer, Aberdeen. In the Tolbooth

Thompson, James 21 years old, labourer, Banff, 5ft 2 5ins, brown hair, sickly. Transported 5 May 1747 from Liverpool to Leeward Islands in *Veteran*, but the ship was attacked off Antigua by a French privateer from Martinique The Governor of Martinique refused English demands to hand the prisoners back, and granted the request of 10 to be sent to France possibly to negotiate for others

Thompson, John Born 18 June 1730, Rathven, Banffshire, son of William Thompson and Margaret Innes 5ft 4 5ins, black hair Resident of Banff Transported 5 May 1747 from Liverpool to Leeward Islands in *Veteran*, but the ship was attacked off Antigua by a French privateer from Martinique The Governor of Martinique refused English demands to hand the prisoners back, and granted the request of 10 to be sent to France possibly to negotiate for others

Thomson, Alexander Sailor, Peterhead.

Thomson, Alexander, of Faichfield, Longside Son of Thomas Thomson of Faichfield (d Nov 1722) aged 67 and Ann Gordon Married with three sons, James, Thomas and John He was exempted from pardon in the Act of Indemnity of 1747

Thomson, James Son to Feichfield, Feichfield, Longside, Aberdeen Joined Rebels with his father

Thomson, James Labourer, Aberdeen Transported

Thomson, John Merchant, Old Aberdeen Lurking after Culloden

Thomson, Thomas, yr of Faichfield Son to Feichfield, Longside, Aberdeen He was probably only a boy at the time of the Rising and compelled to accompany his father to Edinburgh

Tillan, Alexander Horsehirer, Old Aberdeen

Tillan, Alexander Labourer, Kirktoun, Aboyne, Aberdeenshire At Culloden

Tilleray, Andrew Born 24 Sept 1710, Old Machar, Aberdeenshire, son of Andrew Tillery and Margaret Brown Horsehirer, Aberdeen Transported 22 Apr 1747 from Liverpool to Virginia in *Johnson*, arrived Port Oxford, Maryland, 5 Aug 1747

Topp, (or Jopp?) John Carpenter, Banff, aged 16, 5ft 3ins, brown hair, slender, healthy. Transported 5 May 1747 from Liverpool to Leeward Islands in *Veteran*, but the ship was attacked off Antigua by a French privateer from Martinique. The Governor of Martinique refused

English demands to hand the prisoners back, and granted the request of 10 to be sent to France possibly to negotiate for others

Torry, James Dyster, Elgin   Lurking after Culloden

Trail, William Aberdeen   In the Tolbooth

Trail, William Banff   Prisoner at Culloden

Troup, Charles Servant, Pitenkerry, Upper Banchory   At Culloden, but said to be forced out

Troup, William Dancing Master, Aberdeen   Lurking after Culloden

Tulloch, David Farmer, Dunbennan, Huntly   Captain   "He gave great assistance to John Hamilton in raising men for the Prince's army "

Turner, Duncan Candelmore

Turner, John Bricklayer, Aberdeen   Sergeant

Turner, John, yr of Turnerhall Eldest son of John Turner of Turnerhall, Ellon and Margaret Farquharson, his wife   Born in 1725, and from 1741-1745 was at Marischal College, Aberdeen   He married 29 Oct 1757, Elizabeth, daughter of William Urquhart of Meldrum, and had 5 sons and 6 daughters   He died at Beaconsfield, Bucks on 8 Feb 1802, aged 77

Turner, Margaret, of Turnerhall Lady   Daughter of Alexander Farquharson, WS, by his wife, Helen Marshall   She married John Turner of Turnerhall and was mother of John Turner, junior, above   Most active in engaging men for her son   She died 22 Dec 1754

Turner, William Middle Downman, Deskie

Turras, John Smith, Old Meldrum

Tyrie, David Servant, Ellon

Tyrie, David, yr of Dunnydeer In 1704 the Tyries were reported to the Presbytery of Garioch by the minister of Insch as zealous Papists   Those named were John, younger, and Margaret Tulloch his wife, John David James, Anna, Margaret and Bettie, George Gordon and Elspet Tyrie, his wife   The Jacobite David, born in 1727 was son of David Tyrie (d 1750) and his wife, Anna Menzies   He died in Aberdeen, 11 Dec 1807 aged 79

Tyrie, John, Priest Listed as a Popish Priest, Clashmore, and said to have had charge of the school at Scalan for a short time   Probably Uncle to the above David Tyrie, said to have been very active in raising men   He was twice wounded in the head at Culloden, and escaped with great difficulty   He died at Shenval in the Cabrach 19 May 1755

Urquhart, Adam Second son of James Urquhart of Byth, and his wife Jane Porterfield, born in 1721   He was captured on a French ship by the English in Nov 1745, but received a free pardon after trial in London   He spent the next few years as gentleman-in-waiting to Prince Charles   He returned to Scotland, and in 1778 married his cousin Elizabeth, daughter of Capt John Urquhart of Craigston and Cromarty   There were no children   Mrs Urquhart survived her husband and died in 1831, aged 90   He died at Byth on 12 May 1802 aged 80

Urquhart, James Born 1729   Labourer, Aberdeenshire   5ft 5 75ins, brown hair, brown complexion, healthy   At Carlisle garrison   Transported 5 May 1747 from Liverpool to Leeward Islands in *Veteran*, but the ship was attacked off Antigua by a French privateer from Martinique. The Governor of Martinique refused English demands to hand the prisoners back, and granted the request of 10 to be sent to France possibly to negotiate for others

Urquhart, James Aberdeen. Prisoner at Culloden

Urquhart, Kenneth Upper Cults, Banffshire

Volum, James Surgeon. Son of William Volum, sailor, who lived in Harbour Street, Peterhead, and his wife, Ann Strachan. He escaped abroad after Culloden. On his return he married Mary Hay. Died at Peterhead in 1786.

Volum, Thomas Surgeon to the Countess of Erroll, Bowness, Cruden. Brother to James Volum above. He is assumed to have been killed or died during the campaign.

Wales, George Whitefisher in Footdee

Walker, Alexander Born 16 Aug 1723, Bervie Kincardineshire, son of William Walker. Servant. Transported 22 April 1747 from Liverpool to Virginia in *Johnson*, arrived Port Oxford, Maryland 5 Aug 1747

Walker, Alexander Banff. Prisoner at Perth 23 Oct 1746. Enlisted to escape transportation

Walker, Andrew Merchant, Aberdeen. To find caution for good behaviour

Walker, John Aberdeenshire. Prisoner after Culloden

Walker, John Servant, Drumbulg, Aberdeenshire

Walker, William Servant to William Maver, Turriff

Walker, William Wauker, Waukmill Belly, Kincardine. At Falkirk and Culloden

Walker, William Hackhall, Aberdeen

Warren, Robert Born 1727, weaver, Aberdeenshire or Banffshire. Brown hair, 5ft 5ins, well made, healthy. Transported 5 May 1747 from Liverpool to Leeward Islands in *Veteran*, but the ship was attacked off Antigua by a French privateer from Martinique. The Governor of Martinique refused English demands to hand the prisoners back, and granted the request of 10 to be sent to France possibly to negotiate for others.

Watson, George Labourer, Banff. At Carlisle. Transported 22 April 1747 from Liverpool to Virginia in *Johnson*, arrived Port Oxford Maryland, 5 Aug 1747.

Watson, James Merchant, Keith, Banff. Quartermaster in Roy Stuart's Regiment. Was at the Battle of Culloden and there killed.

Watson, Thomas Servant, Elgin. Drummer to Jacobites. Lurking after Culloden.

Watt, John Born Feb 1724, son of John Watt. Fisherman, Gamrie, Banffshire. Transported 22 April 1747 from Liverpool to Virginia in *Johnson*, arrived Port Oxford, Maryland, 5 Aug 1747

Watt, John Servant, Gamry, Banff. Lurking after Culloden

Watt, William Auchmedin, Aberdeen. Lurking after Culloden.

Weaver, William Aberdeenshire. Prisoner at Inverness.

Webster, James Servant, Balnaboth, Birse. At Culloden, but said to be forced out.

Weir, George Workman, Loanhead, Old Machar

White, Alexander Hookmaker, Aberdeen   Lurking after Culloden

White, Alexander, jun in Ardlawhill His father was John White of Ardlawhill, son of Captain Alexander White, a Knight of Windsor   He survived the Rising and in November 1748 was in Paris   He had a sister, Elizabeth White (who married George Keith of Northfield) and who was served co-heir with him to their father in 1758

White, Daniel Hookmaker, Aberdeen   Lurking after Culloden

White, George Mill of Gask, Turriff

Whyte, ... Divinity Student, Presbytery of Deer   He escaped cries for his execution, but was denied a licence to practice his profession from 2 Apr 1746   If he survived the '45, it may be concluded he may have embarked on another profession

Wight, Harry Was member of garrison bringing Spanish arms from Peterhead

Wilkie, Sanders Aberdeen   Prisoner

Wilkin, Alexander Farmer, Kinharrachy, Ellon

Wilkins, Joseph Weaver, Old Aberdeen

Williamson, Alexander Croft of Minmore

Williamson, John Born 1730, labourer, resident in Angus or Aberdeenshire   5ft 3 75ins light brown, thin   Transported 5 May 1747 from Liverpool to Leeward Islands in *Veteran*, but the ship was attacked off Antigua by a French privateer from Martinique   The Governor of Martinique refused English demands to hand the prisoners back, and granted the request of 10 to be sent to France possibly to negotiate for others

Williamson, William Salmon fisher, Hillhead Blairs, Maryculter, Kincardine   At Culloden and prisoner in Aberdeen

Wilson, Alexander Servant to Sir William Gordon of Park Bannfshire

Wilson, David Servant to Sir William Gordon of Park, Gardenhead Park, Banffshire   Forced out by his master and at home after Culloden

Wilson, John Labourer, Kennethmont

Wilson, Robert Wright, Fochabers, Moray   Deserted Jacobites in England

Wilson, William Servant to William Maver, Keith or Turriff   Assisted in robbing James Paterson, carrier of the Laird of Grant's letter

Wilson, William Tailor of Ellon   He made some of the clothes for the Highlanders and followed them north for payment

Wilson, William Farmer, Kirkhill, Ellon

Wishart, James Banff, Labourer   Carlisle garrison, pardoned on condition of enlistment

Wishart, William Prisoner in Tolboth, Aberdeen

Withols, Isobel Aberdeen   Followed Lord Pitsligo's Regiment

Wood, Andrew Born in Strathbogie on 17 Jan 24, of respectable parents and had a good education   He was offered a commission by Colonel Roy Stuart   He was taken at Culloden and from Inverness was shipped to London   He was executed on 28 November 1746 aged 22, and made a dying speech which was printed in the "Lyon in Mourning"

Wood, David Born 1699, labourer Resident in Kinneff, Kincardineshire. Transported 24 February 1747 from Liverpool to Virginia in *Gildart*, arrived Port North Potomac, Maryland, 5 Aug 1747.

Wotherspoon, or Witherspoon, John Minister and DD of Aberdeen Known to have taken part in the Rising. He afterwards went to America, where he became a prominent member of the Whig party, and was the only clergyman to sign "the Declaration of Independence." he died in 1794, aged 71.

Wright, Alexander Sub-tenant, Glengerach, Banff Said to be hired out Lurking after Culloden.

Wright, John Tailor, Strathbogie, said to · hired by the inhabitants Lurking after Culloden.

Wyer, John Prisoner after Culloden Deserter from the Royal Scots

Yates, Francis Resident in Fochabers, Morayshire Transported 24 Feb 1747 from Liverpool to Virginia in *Gildart*, arrived Port North Potomac, Maryland, 5 Aug 1747

Yates, William Weaver, Clunybeg, Banffshire In Carlisle garrison Transported 1747

Yates, William Labourer, Fochabers In Carlisle garrison

Yeates, William Weaver, Clunybeggs, Banffshire Transported 22 April 1747 from Liverpool to Virginia in *Johnson*, arrived Port North Potomac, Maryland, 5 Aug 1747

Young, Magnus Aberdeen Monaltrie's Regiment, prisoner at Culloden

www.ingramcontent.com/pod-product-compliance
Lightning Source LLC
Chambersburg PA
CBHW070928270326
41927CB00011B/2775